Picking Up the Pieces

by Piecemakers

Favour is deceitful and beauty is vain: but a woman that feareth the Lord, she shall be praised. Give her the fruit of her hands; and let her own works praise her in the gates.

Proverbs 31:30–31

INTERNATIONAL

95 Mayhill Street
Saddle Brook, New Jersey

A special thank you to Sandy Schner for his constant prodding to begin this project; Chuck Sabosik from EZ International for his confidence in us to complete it; and to all the Piecemakers for creating, sewing, quilting and generally supporting the entire effort.

Great is our God and greatly to be praised.

Acknowledgments

Photography: Paul Saunders of Paul Saunders Photography, San Juan Capistrano, California.

Graphic Designers: Mimi and John Shimp of SPPS, Inc., Las Vegas, Nevada.

Machine quilting technique used in our *"No Stress" Vest* is adapted from an article by Bird Ross in "Threads" Magazine, No. 40, April/May 1992, Copyright 1992, Taunton Press. Used with permission.

Gail Abeloe from Back Porch Press for use of her "Heartwarming Jacket" pattern as the basic body for the "Presidential Platform 1992" jacket. Used with permission.

Pen and ink sketches by Piecemakers.

ISBN: 1-881588-02-5.

Printed in USA.

Table of Contents

Dear Quilters,

This book is not written as a strip-piecing method book but as a pattern book chocked full of new designs to spark the creativity and interest of everyone from beginning to advanced quilters. For that reason, we have included fully strip-pieced designs, quilts that have a combination of stripping and template-making, and still others with a touch of appliqué to soften the look and entice quiltmakers who love handwork as well as machine sewing.

Some of the patterns are so simply beautiful that someone who has never made a quilt before can successfully complete a first project. Others present a challenge that will encourage veteran quiltmakers to explore variations never even imagined by the designers of the patterns.

Please embrace these designs, play with them, expand them, change them and – if you feel so inclined – send us pictures of what you have done. We will be eager to see what you have created!

This book hopefully is a springboard for you to further journey into the wonderful world of quilting. We have inherited a precious art and expression of beauty from our foremothers (and fathers!) and want to be able to pass it on as freely as it was given from our Creator.

Happy quiltmaking and may the God of Abraham, Isaac and Jacob richly bless you all.

The Piecemakers

General Instructions
&
EZ Tool Mini-Tutorial

Introduction

This book has been written so that anyone with four basic tools – a rotary cutter, mat, 6" x 24" ruler with angles, and plastic or cardboard for making templates – can pick up the book and make the quilts. Along with these basics are a vast array of tools from EZ International that can make the cutting process even easier. Either way you should be successful creating the projects in this book.

Part of the fun of books like *Picking Up the Pieces* is the opportunity to experiment with new tools. The next few pages will be concerned with the rules for cutting with the "basic four" (Rules to Cut By) and instructions for using the EZ tools. If you use the EZ International tools rather than regular strip cutting methods, remember to follow the instructions in the EZ Tool Tutorial section. We have indicated with an asterisk, places in the patterns where these specific tools can be used. **You will need to use the size strips appropriate for those tools instead of the size strips indicated on the Cutting the Strips chart.**

Once you've chosen a project, please read through the instructions thoroughly before beginning. This should save you some time and frustration if you are familiar with all the steps at the outset.

We hope you have as much fun creating with these patterns as we have!

Getting Prepared

Supplies Needed

For piecing the quilt top:

Rotary cutter

Mat for rotary cutter

6" x 24" acrylic ruler with ⅛" markings and 45° angle marked

Sewing machine

Thread – one color to blend with your fabrics

Seam ripper – always good to have just in case!

#1 extra-soft pencil or graphite pencil to mark light to medium fabrics

Silver or white pencil for marking dark fabric

Straight pins

Cardboard or Temp-A-Graphs™   Easy Angle™

Easy Angle II™   Easy Eight™

Companion Angle™   SPEED GRIDS®

Quickline Ruler®   Second Cut Ruler

Draft 'n Cut Ruler   Quilt Clips™

For hand appliqué:

Thread to match each fabric being appliquéd

Piecemakers® Hand Appliqué needles

Scissors

For hand quilting:

Round or oval quilting hoop – make sure it is good quality with nice smooth edges

Piecemakers® Quilting/Betweens needles

¼" wide masking tape – for quilting ¼" away from seam lines

Quilting stencils – for marking designs in borders and other portions of the quilt top

Quilting thread

Thimble

For hand tying:

Size 3 Perle cotton thread

Piecemakers® Chenille or 3½" Dollmaking needles

Needle grabber – you may purchase one or use a large broccoli rubber band

Choosing Your Fabrics

Beauty is in the eye of the beholder. However, confidence in choosing fabrics is something that usually comes with practice and experimenting.

To choose fabrics for any of the projects in this book, we will list a few basic guidelines to help you:

1. Decide the color family or families you want to work with.

2. Find a fabric you can't live without on which to build your quilt. Preferably it should contain hues of some or all the colors you're working with.

3. Choose fabrics in dark, medium and light tones to contrast with each other. Sometimes you may be working primarily with pastels or with bright bold colors, but the key is CONTRAST.

4. Choose a variety of sizes and types of prints – solids, stripes, plaids and checks, large florals, small calicos, tone on tone prints and widely-spaced prints. This step probably adds the most interest to your quilt.

5. Don't disregard a fabric just because it isn't one of your favorites. Sometimes it ends up being the fabric that pulls everything together or bridges a gap.

6. Stand away from your selection to get an overall view. If a particular fabric isn't going to work, you can usually see it when you back away.

7. Follow your instincts. You'll find that you know more than you think you do about coordinating colors.

Fabric Preparation

Pre-shrink and iron all fabrics before working with them. We recommend soaking fabrics in cold water and drying them in a warm dryer. Make sure there are no "bleeders" before drying them.

You can treat bleeders by soaking them in white vinegar and then rinsing them *thoroughly*. If this does not stop the bleeding, then try your laundry detergent and put the fabric through a wash cycle. A fabric still bleeding after this process may need to be retired and another found to take its place!

Choosing Your Quilt Size

All of the patterns in this book are 12" finished blocks. They were created so that several blocks can be put together to form interesting designs without the use of lattice strips. The exception is "Flying High", which has lattice strips as part of the quilt design.

Each pattern contains its own sizing and yardage chart to make it easy for you to choose a quilt size and purchase fabrics for your project.

Rules to Cut By

We have done all the figuring for you in the patterns in this book. However, for those patterns that you may run across which do not use the quick-strip method, the following rules will come in very handy.

Squares and Rectangles

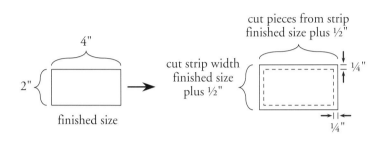

These are cut from a strip ½" larger than the finished size of one side (the shorter side of a rectangle or the side of a square). This allows for a ¼" seam allowance.

Example: For a 2" finished square, cut strips 2½" wide and divide into squares.

Example: For a 2" x 4" finished rectangle, cut strip 2½" wide and divide at 4½" intervals.

Right Triangles with Two Equal Sides *

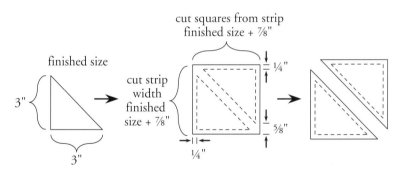

These are cut from a strip ⅞" larger than the finished triangle.

Example: For a finished 3" triangle, cut strip 3⅞" wide. Divide the strip into squares and then slice the squares diagonally into triangles.

*Easy Angle™ can be used for these triangles. Refer to page 18 for instructions.

Right Triangles with Unequal Sides

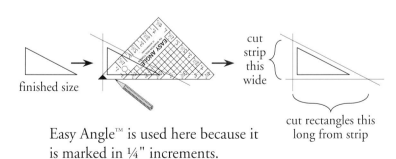

Easy Angle™ is used here because it is marked in ¼" increments.

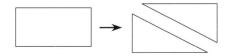

Start by making a template including seam allowances to get the measurement for cutting strips.

Then, measure the height of the short side, including seam allowances, to determine the width for cutting strips.

Next, measure the length of the longer side, including seam allowances to get the measurement for dividing the strips. Divide strips into rectangles of that measurement.

Slice rectangles diagonally into triangles.

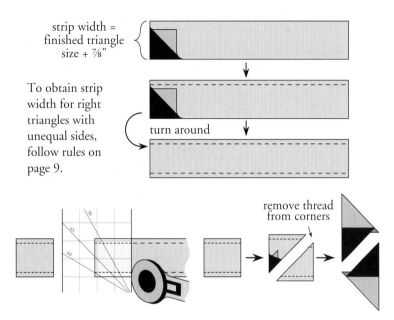

strip width =
finished triangle
size + ⅞"

To obtain strip
width for right
triangles with
unequal sides,
follow rules on
page 9.

turn around

remove thread
from corners

Right triangles with equal sides or unequal sides can be sewn and cut according to this technique:

Sew two strips right sides together, down one side, and then turn the strip around to sew the other side. This way you will sew the two seams in opposite directions and keep the strips from "bowing".

Divide the strips into squares (or rectangles). Slice into triangles. Open and you will have two pieced triangles as shown at left. Press seam toward darker fabric.

45° Diamonds *

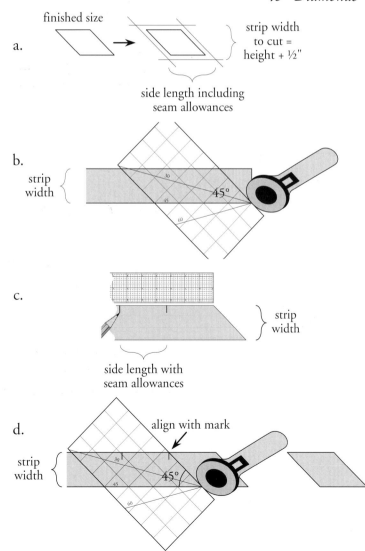

a.

finished size

strip width
to cut =
height + ½"

side length including
seam allowances

b.

strip
width

45°

c.

strip
width

side length with
seam allowances

d.

strip
width

align with mark

45°

These are used for eight-pointed stars. Make a template including seam allowances to get the measurement for cutting strips.

Measure height of diamond as shown, including seam allowances, to determine width to cut strips. (See Diagram a.)

Measure one side of the diamond, including seam allowances, to get the measurement for dividing the strips into diamonds. (See Diagram a.)

Lay the 45° line of the ruler on the strip and cut the corner off the strip. (See Diagram b.)

Lay ruler along top of strip and mark off at the intervals you measured above – side length including seam allowances. (See Diagram c.)

Lay ruler on strip with the 45° line along the bottom edge of the strip and the edge aligned at the point marked. Slice. Continue slicing on each marked point. (See Diagram d.) *Or use Easy Eight™ for the diamonds. Refer to page 20 for instructions.

Quick-Pieced Triangles *

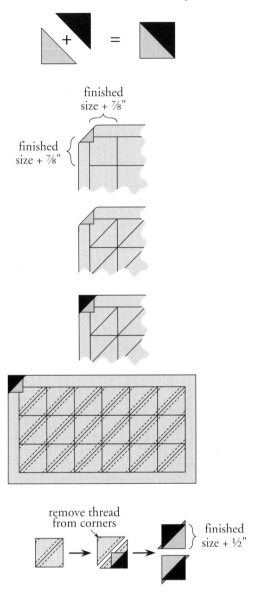

finished
size + ⅞"

finished
size + ⅞"

remove thread
from corners

finished
size + ½"

These are drawn and sewn before they are cut. Use the following method when you need several pairs of triangles pieced together.

Draw a grid on one fabric with squares that are ⅞" larger than the finished triangle you want. For example, if you want 3" finished triangles, draw squares 3⅞". The grid should have half as many squares as triangles needed.

Draw diagonal lines through the squares of the grid.

Place the two fabrics right sides together, pinning enough to anchor.

Stitch ¼" on either side of the diagonal lines. Cut apart on straight and diagonal drawn lines.

Pull apart triangle pairs at tips and press.

*An alternative to creating your own grid is to use SPEED GRIDS®. Refer to page 21.

Criss-Cross Triangles *

Right triangles with two equal sides sometimes need to be cut with the long side (hypotenuse) on the straight of grain. To do this, measure the height of the finished triangle, double that number and then add 1¼". This gives you the size strip to cut. Next, divide the strip into squares and criss-cross slice into triangles. This is a criss-cross slice as shown.

*Companion Angle could also be used to cut these triangles.

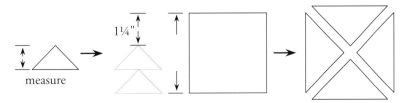

measure

1¼"

General Guidelines

Cutting Strips

When we talk about cutting strips, we always mean selvage to selvage – the width of the fabric.

Yardages

Because of the quick cutting methods, you may occasionally have a few extra pieces. We have allowed one extra strip for cutting errors, except for wide strips.

Dividing and Slicing Strips

We recommend keeping your strips folded in half crosswise for slicing into smaller pieces. This saves time and in some cases it will insure reverse cuts of pieces that are not symmetrical. We will tell you specifically if you need to slice a strip opened instead of folded.

Cutting Strips Wider Than 6"

When you need to cut strips wider than 6", use one of the following methods to cut.

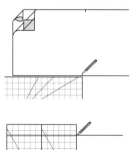

Method 1: Turn a 6" x 24" ruler sideways and measure. Make small marks at the desired measurement at each end of your fabric. Turn the ruler longways, align with marks and then cut.

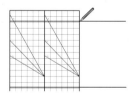

Method 2: Use two rulers side by side to get the measurement you need.

Seam Allowances

Seam allowances of ¼" ARE ALREADY INCLUDED in all cutting instructions, whether you are strip cutting or using a template. The only exceptions are hand appliqué patterns, which are explained in the specific projects.

Pressing

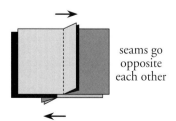

seams go opposite each other

Seam allowances are always pressed closed to one side, never open. Usually they are pressed toward the dark fabric. At seam intersections, press seams opposite to one another.

It is much quicker to assembly line and chain sew your units in the blocks together. For example, let's say you are sewing thirty blocks for a quilt. Cut out all pieces as instructed and lay the pieces stacked thirty to a pile in the shape of your block.

If you were ready to piece the B/C unit, you would sew all of those units at the same time, chaining them through your machine without cutting the threads. This is a huge time and thread saver. As a bonus, you only have to think through each step once! Just be sure you do it right so you don't have to rip out thirty pieces! Cut apart and press after sewing.

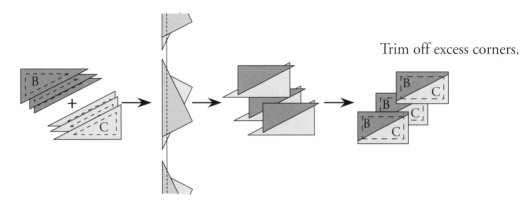

Trim off excess corners.

Reading the "Cutting the Strips" Chart

After reading through all directions for a project, go back to "Cutting the Strips". Using the Fabric #, Size of Strip, and Number of Strips columns, cut the strips indicated for your selected quilt size. (See sample chart below.)

Sometimes, fabric numbers or pattern pieces will not be on the chart. This is because they are quick-pieced triangles or single templates which are explained and charted in the directions for the project.

In the directions, when you are instructed to cut squares, triangles, etc. from the strips, refer to the Total Pieces Needed column to find out how many of a particular shape to cut.

Cutting the Strips

Quilt	Fabric #	Pattern Piece	Size of Strip	Number of Strips	Total Pieces Needed
Wall	1	A	4½"	2	18
	1	B	3¾"	1	18
	2	A	4½"	2	18
	2	B	3¾"	1	18
	1st Border	-	2"	6	-
	2nd Border	-	4½"	6	-

Sewing the Quilt Top Together

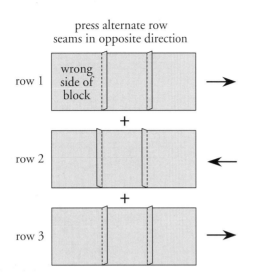

press alternate row
seams in opposite direction

row 1

wrong side of block

+

row 2

+

row 3

Refer to the Yardage Chart for each specific project to find the number of blocks per row and the number of rows for the size quilt you are making.

Sew together blocks for rows first. Lay rows in order face down. Pick up the first row and press the seams toward the right. Pick up the second row and press the seams toward the left. Continue to alternate directions of the rows as you press.

Sew rows together.

Adding the Borders

Refer to the Yardage Chart of the specific project for the number of borders and border sizes. Cut the number of border strips indicated on the "Cutting the Strips" chart. Always cut the strips selvage to selvage of your fabric.

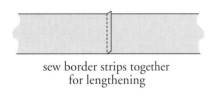

sew border strips together
for lengthening

To make border strips long enough for each side of your quilt, sew enough strips together to be a little longer than the finished length or width of the quilt. For example, if your quilt will be finished 94" x 108", sew 3 strips together for the length and 2½ strips together for the width of the quilt.

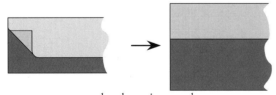

sew border strips together
for multiple borders

Next, if you have multiple borders, sew the border strips for each side to each other before attaching to the quilt top.

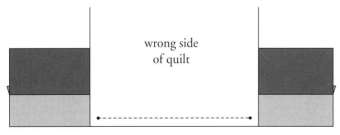

wrong side
of quilt

Before sewing on the borders,
mark a dot on each corner of the
quilt ¼" in from the edges.

To attach to the quilt top, find the middle of a border strip and match that point to the middle of the appropriate quilt side. Pin the border strip to the quilt, right sides together. Sew with a ¼" seam allowance, beginning ¼" from one corner and ending ¼" from the next corner.

wrong side
of quilt

Continue to sew each strip on in this way. Press all the borders toward the outside of the quilt. Turn the quilt top face down and straighten everything as shown.

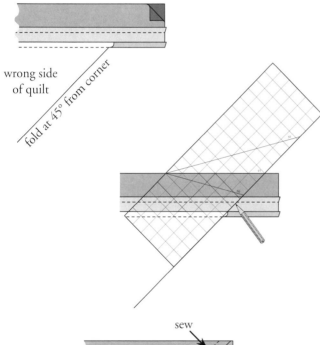

wrong side
of quilt

fold at 45° from corner

Fold the corner of the quilt diagonally, lining up adjacent border strips. Lay the 45° line of your ruler along the top edge of the border with the edge of the ruler at the point where the borders attach to the quilt. Draw a line along the edge of the ruler.

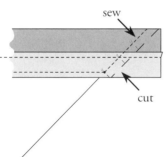

sew

cut

Pin (especially where border seams meet each other) and sew on the drawn line, being careful not to catch the little corner of your quilt top. This seam is a 45° angle from the corner of the quilt top.

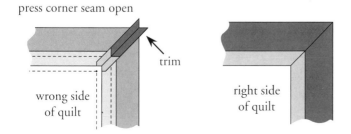

press corner seam open

trim

wrong side
of quilt

right side
of quilt

Cut excess fabric to a ½" seam allowance and press open.

Finishing Your Quilt

Marking and Basting

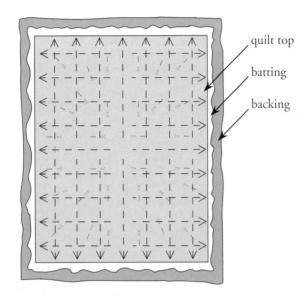

quilt top

batting

backing

If quilting, mark the top where necessary with a fabric marking pencil. Quilting stencils make this step very easy. Baste your top, batting and backing together, making a "sandwich". Use the floor, a large table or a frame to baste the quilt. Tape the back, face down, to the floor or table making sure it is pulled taut. Your back should be at least 2" larger than your top all around.

Center batting on top of back and then center quilt top on batting. Pin from the center out, continually smoothing layers. Baste from the center out. Basting stitches should be approximately 1" long and rows should be no more that six inches apart; don't pull basting stitches so tight that they pucker.

Quilting

We often quilt "in the ditch" around the individual pieces OR ¼" away from the seams. Larger areas lend themselves nicely to a pretty quilting design. Refer 3to page 7 for tools you'll need for quilting.

To quilt your quilt, place your basted quilt in a hoop making sure all layers are smooth. Do not pull the quilt taut in the hoop – leave some play. It makes quilting easier.

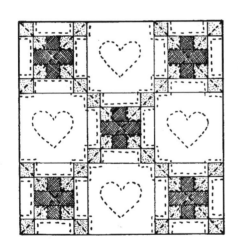

Enlargement – Top View.

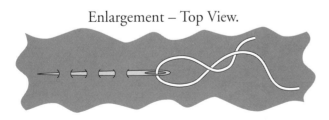

Side View.

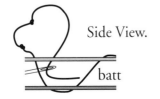

batt

Cut your quilting thread approximately 18" long. Always hide the knots at the beginning and the end of threads. Make a small knot in one end of the thread which you pull through the fabric into the batting. Back stitch to secure it.

Quilt with small even stitches. You can load your needle with 3 or 4 stitches at a time. See figure at the left.

When ending a thread, tie 2 small knots in the thread near the surface of the quilt, take a small backstitch and pull the knots into the batting. Clip the thread at the surface of the quilt.

Tying

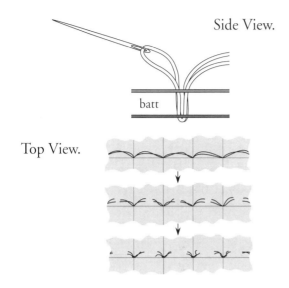

Side View.

batt

Top View.

We recommend using DMC Perle Cotton #3 and Piecemakers® Chenille needles to tie your quilt. Look at the pattern and decide where it would be appropriate to tie. Every 4" to 6" is a good distance.

Cut long strands and tie with a doubled thread. Run the thread through several squares. Then clip and tie them. See diagram at the left.

After tying the quilt, trim the threads to the length you desire, usually about 1".

Binding

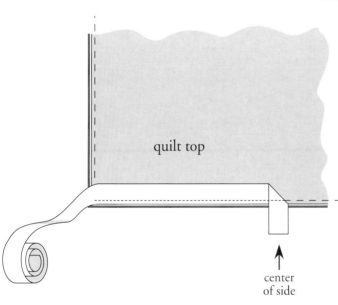

quilt top

center of side

Begin with a bias strip cut 2½" wide. Iron strip in half, WRONG sides together. Stay-stitch raw edges together with a scant ¼"seam allowance.

Trim quilt batting and backing even or just a scant bit bigger than the top. If you haven't quilted right up to the edge, baste it down all the way around to keep it from shifting while you sew.

Begin at the middle of one side of the quilt to apply binding. Match raw edge of binding to raw edge of quilt, leaving about 5" of binding free at the beginning. Fold the tail at an angle as shown.

Stitch, using a ¼" seam until you come to the first corner.

Stop ¼" from the edge; backstitch and cut your thread. DO NOT CUT BINDING!

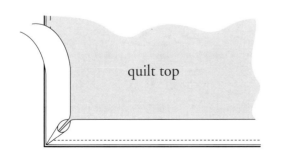

quilt top

Form a pleat in the binding ¼" tall. Leave the pleat free (i. e., don't stitch it down), and pivot the quilt. Put the machine needle down in the same ¼" place where you stopped, but along the second side. Stitch along the second side of the quilt.

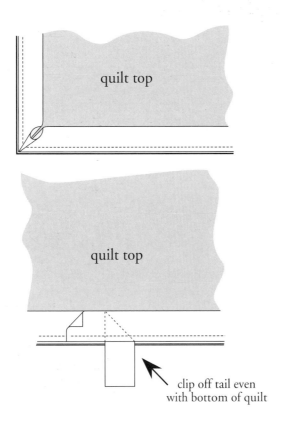

clip off tail even
with bottom of quilt

Repeat the same process on each corner of the quilt.

Continue stitching binding until you overlap the tail you started with. Clip excess binding off. Also clip tail even with edge of quilt.

Turn binding to the back of the quilt and blindstitch just over the machine stitching line. (Your corners should automatically make a nice mitered pleat.)

Washing Your Quilt

Over the years we have washed many quilts and would like to pass along some tips to you. These methods have worked very well for us, but we don't pretend to be an absolute authority on the subject, so if you have a valuable quilt or one you feel might need special handling, please call a textile museum.

All quilts should be washed with care – think of all the time you put into making the quilt. Only wash a quilt when necessary – it doesn't need to be laundered every time with the sheets! When you do wash it, use cold water and a mild soap. We use Orvus Paste or Ensure (made for quilts by Mountain Mist). If you use Orvus Paste (used in museums for fine textiles), mix 1 tablespoon in a cup of water and add to the rest of the the water. If the quilt is in good shape and you have used polyester, a cotton/poly blend batt or a wool batt, you can launder your quilt in the machine, but no agitation! We go to the laundromat and use the front loading machines that tumble –

GUIDELINES

Cold Water

No Agitation

Mild Soap

Lay flat to dry

they don't agitate. To dry – lay a large sheet or several big towels on the floor and lay the quilt flat on top. If you put it in the dryer, wrinkles tend to set in.

If you have an older, more fragile quilt, or have used a 100% cotton batt, it is best to hand wash in your bathtub. Once again, use cold water and Ensure, Orvus Paste, or a balanced PH shampoo. Gently press on it (yes, you can use your feet!) to remove the dirt, but never wring or twist it. Rinse several times, then roll it in towels to get the excess moisture out. It will be quite wet, so you should change the sheet or towels and turn it over once in a while until it is dry.

Direct sunlight is not good for fabrics. It will quickly fade them and will weaken the fibers, so be sure you protect your quilts and enjoy them for many years to come!

When storing a quilt, don't put them in plastic because they need to breathe.

18

Using Easy Angle™ and Easy Angle II™

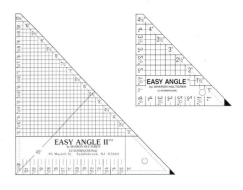

The Easy Angle™ and Easy Angle II™ make cutting triangles with equal sides a snap. As a bonus, it also makes fast and accurate squares from the same size strip as the triangles.

The Easy Angle™ is for triangles in the range of 1" to 4½" while the Easy Angle II™ has the range of 3" to 10½". Both tools are used the same way.

Step-by-Step Instructions:

Step 1: Determine your finished triangle size. Add ½" to get your unfinished triangle size.

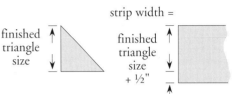

strip width =

finished triangle size

finished triangle size + ½"

Step 2: Cut the fabric strip the size of your unfinished triangle. For example, a 2" finished triangle would need a fabric strip of 2½".

Step 3: Lay fabric strip on the cutting mat in up to four layers, right sides together. Straighten the end of fabric strip by using the square corner of the tool and slicing.

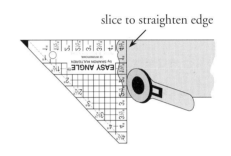

slice to straighten edge

Step 4: Turn tool so the words "Easy Angle™" read right side up and the black tip of the tool is at the right bottom corner.

Step 5: Align the bottom of tool on the bottom edge of the fabric and slide until the dashed line is at the top left corner of fabric. (Your unfinished triangle size should also line up on the bottom and top left grid marks.) Slice along diagonal side.

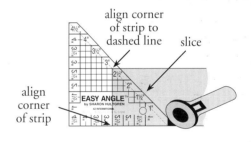

align corner of strip to dashed line

slice

align corner of strip

Step 6: Take the square corner of tool and flip over so the corner is now at the top right. (The words "Easy Angle™" are now reversed, but the black tip of the tool remains at the bottom right side.)

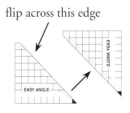

flip across this edge

Step 7: Align the left diagonal edge of the tool to the cut fabric edge and slide until the black tip hangs over the bottom fabric edge. (Your unfinished triangle size should also line up on the left and right top grid marks.) Slice along straight side.

Step 8: Continue steps 4 through 7 until you have made all your triangles.

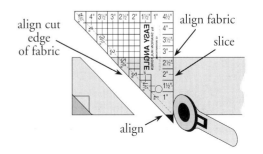

align cut edge of fabric

align fabric

slice

align

Using Companion Angle™

The Companion Angle™ is a quick and accurate way to make the long edge of a triangle with equal sides on the straight of the grain to prevent distortion on the outside of a block, border or quilt.

Step-by-Step Instructions:

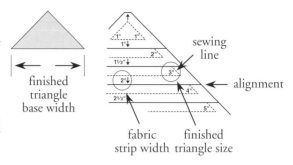

Step 1: Determine the required size of the long edge of your finished triangle.

Step 2: Align the tool so that the words "Companion Angle™" can be read. The dashed lines represent sewing lines and show the finished triangle size, based on a ¼" seam allowance; center numbers represent the width of the strip to cut and solid lines underneath are used for alignment. (For example, cut a 2" strip for a finished 3" triangle.) Cut your fabric strip to the correct size using a ruler.

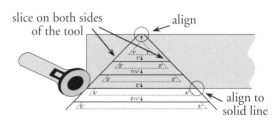

Step 3: Align tool with edge of strip. Carefully slice on both sides of the tool.

Step 4: Turn the tool so the words "Companion Angle™" read are upside down.

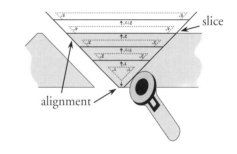

Step 5: Align tool with edge of strip. Carefully slice on both sides of the tool.

Step 6: Continue steps 3 through 5 until you have cut all your triangles.

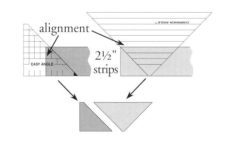

Use Companion Angle™ with the Easy Angle™ or Easy Angle II™ to get perfectly compatible triangles. Simply use the same width strips and line up with equivalent alignments. For example, 2½" strips would require aligning fabric using the 2½" lines on both tools.

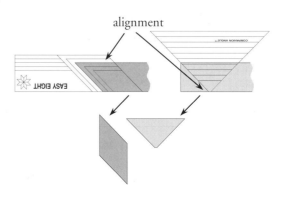

Use Companion Angle™ with the Easy Eight™ to get perfectly matching pieces. Use the same width strips and align the Companion Angle™ top with the strip edge.

Using Easy Eight™

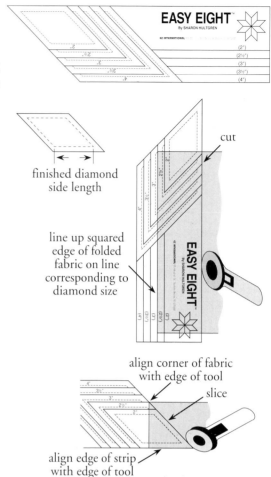

The Easy Eight™ takes the difficulty out of making diamonds used in eight-pointed stars. It will make diamonds with seam allowances in sizes from 1" to 4" without templates or marking.

Step-by-Step Instructions:

Step 1: Determine the length of a side of your finished diamond.

Step 2: Use the numbers in parenthesis and the straight grid marks on the tool as a ruler to cut your fabric strip, but do not use a standard ruler because the tool grid will automatically convert the finished diamond to the correct fabric strip size. Fold fabric if necessary and cut.

Step 3: Turn the tool so the diamond grids are on the right and the numbers are readable.

Step 4: Trim the excess triangle off the left side of strip by aligning the bottom fabric edge and sliding until the top corner of the fabric is lined with the tool. Slice.

Step 5: Slide the tool to the right until the solid black diamond grid fits all around the top and cut edge of the fabric strip. Slice.

Step 6: Continue repeating step 5 until you have cut all your diamonds.

Using SPEED GRIDS®

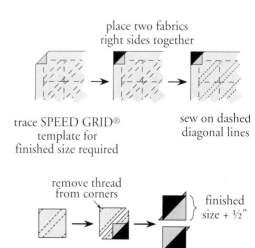

Quick-pieced triangles can be simplified by using the SPEED GRIDS®. They are available in ½", 1", 2", and 3" finished sizes.

Step-by-Step Instructions:

Step 1: Use the grid to trace the lines on the wrong side of your first fabric.

Step 2: Place the two fabrics right sides together and sew along the dashed diagonal lines.

Step 3: Using a ruler and a rotary cutter, cut on the solid lines and between the dashed lines.

Step 4: Pick apart sewn corners and open at sewn line to form a quick-pieced triangle.

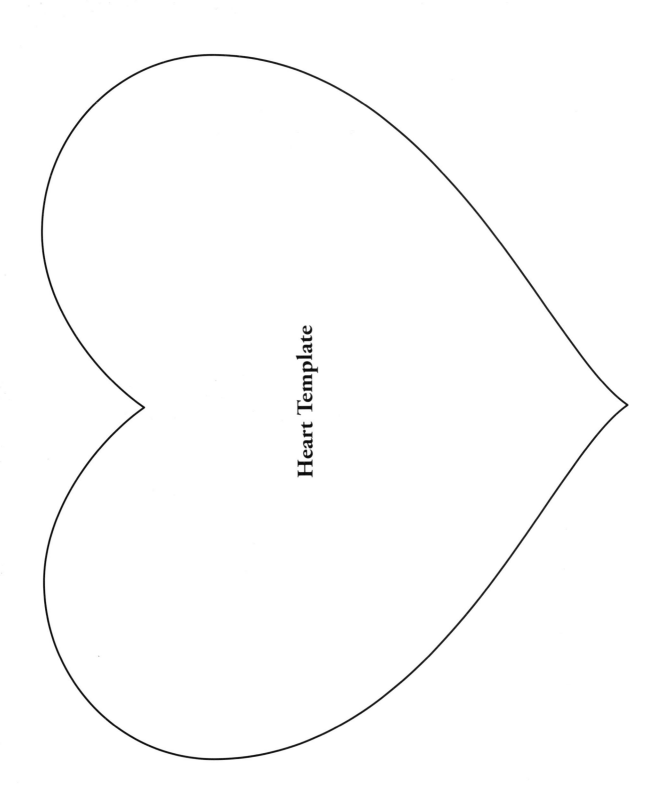

Heart Template

This template can be used with the Crossing Over pattern on page 24.

Projects

The Lord thy God shall bless thee in all thine increase, and in all the works of thine hands, therefore thou shalt surely rejoice.
Deuteronomy 16:15

Crossing Over

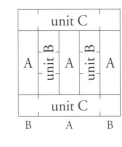

Crossing Over is a delightful "beginner-beginner's" quilt that is all strip cut with blank blocks in between. As a variation to the quilt pictured on page 53, appliqué hearts on the blank blocks as shown here. This pattern needs to have an odd number of rows and blocks per row to complete the design.

See photograph page 53.

Fabric #1

Fabric #2

Fabric #3

Yardage Chart					
	Wall **5 x 5**	**Twin** **3 x 7**	**Double** **5 x 7**	**Queen** **5 x 7**	**King** **7 x 9**
Fabric#					
1 (background)	2½	2½	3½	3½	6⅛
2 (chain)	⅞	1	1⅛	1⅛	1¾
3 (center)	⅔	⅝	1	1	1¼
Borders (finished sizes given)					
1st Border	2½" – ¾	4" – 1½	3½"– 1¼	4½" – 1⅔	5" – 1⅛ (sides only)
2nd Border	1" – ⅜	2" – ⅞	2" – ⅞	3" – 1¼	3" – 1⅓
3rd Border	2½" – ¾	4" – 1⅔ (top & bottom) 6" (sides)	3½" – 1¼	4½" – 1⅔	-
Batting	4½	6⅛	6⅛	6¼	9
Back	4½	6⅛	6⅛	8	9
Binding	1	1	1	1	1¼
Finished Size	72" x 72"	60" x 104"	78" x 102"	84" x 108"	100" x 114"
No. of Pieced Blocks	13	11	18	18	32
No. of Blank Blocks	12	10	17	17	31

				Cutting the Strips		
Quilt	Fabric #	Pattern Piece	Size of Strip	Number of Strips	Total Pieces Needed
Wall	1	A	7⅝"	4	52
	1	D	12½"	4	12
	2	B	2⅞"	8	104
	3	A	7⅝"	2	26
	3	B	2⅞"	1	13
	1st Border	-	3"	8	-
	2nd Border	-	1½"	8	-
	3rd Border	-	3"	8	-
Twin	1	A	7⅝"	4	44
	1	D	12½"	4	10
	2	B	2⅞"	10	88
	3	A	7⅝"	2	22
	3	B	2⅞"	1	11
	1st Border	-	4½"	9	-
	2nd Border	-	2½"	9	-
	3rd Border (Top & Bottom)	-	4½"	3	-
	3rd Border (Sides)	-	6½"	6	-
Double	1	A	7⅝"	6	72
	1	D	12½"	6	17
	2	B	2⅞"	12	144
	3	A	7⅝"	3	36
	3	B	2⅞"	2	18
	1st Border	-	4"	10	-
	2nd Border	-	2½"	10	-
	3rd Border	-	4"	10	-
Queen	1	A	7⅝"	6	72
	1	D	12½"	6	17
	2	B	2⅞"	12	144
	3	A	7⅝"	3	36
	3	B	2⅞"	2	18
	1st Border	-	5"	11	-
	2nd Border	-	3½"	11	-
	3rd Border	-	5"	11	-
King	1	A	7⅝"	10	128
	1	D	12½"	11	31
	2	B	2⅞"	20	256
	3	A	7⅝"	6	64
	3	B	2⅞"	3	32
	1st Border (sides only)	-	5½"	6	-
	2nd Border	-	3½"	12	-

Cutting and Sewing the Pieces

Cut the strips indicated on the "Cutting the Strips" chart.

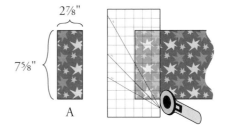

A Pieces. Divide the 7⅝" strips of fabric #3 into rectangles every 2⅞"and set aside.

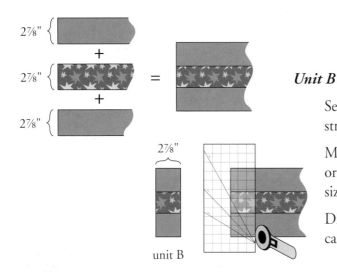

Unit B

Sew two 2⅞" strips of fabric #2 and one 2⅞" strip of fabric #3 together as shown at the left.

Make two sets of strips for the wall and twin sizes, or make three sets for the double through king sizes.

Divide the sets every 2⅞". These pieces are called Unit **B**. Set aside.

Unit C

Unit **C** is made of one **A** piece and two **B** pieces.

Sew one 7⅝" strip of fabric #1 and two 2⅞" strips of fabric #2 as follows:

Make two sets of Unit **C** for the wall and twin sizes, or make three sets for the double through king sizes.

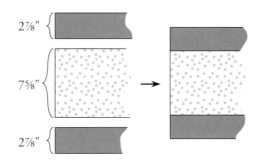

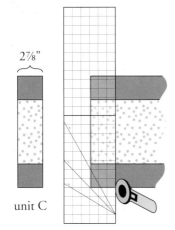

Divide the sets every 2⅞".

These pieces are called Unit **C**. Set aside.

More A Pieces. Take the 7⅝" strips that are left of fabric #1 and divide them into rectangles every 2⅞". Set aside.

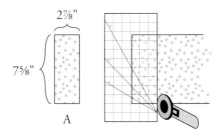

D Pieces. Divide the 12½" strips of fabric #1 into squares. Set aside.

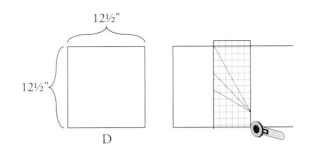

D

Assembling the Block

1. Sew Unit **B**'s to either side of **A** pieces.

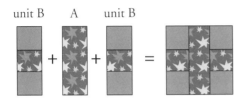

unit B   A   unit B

2. Add **A** pieces to either side of the squares formed in step 1.

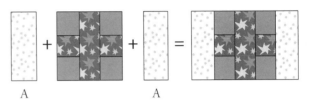

A   A

3. Add Unit **C**'s to the top and bottom of unit formed in step 2 to complete the block.

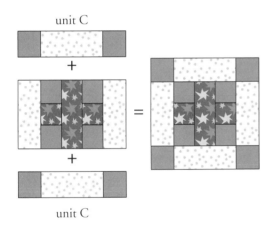

unit C

unit C

Constructing the Quilt Top

Sew blocks together into rows first. Refer to the Yardages chart for the number of blocks across and down for each size. After making all the rows, sew them together as shown, matching seams. (Refer to the graphic to the right.)

Follow the "Sewing the Quilt Top Together" section on pages 14-15 to complete your quilt top.

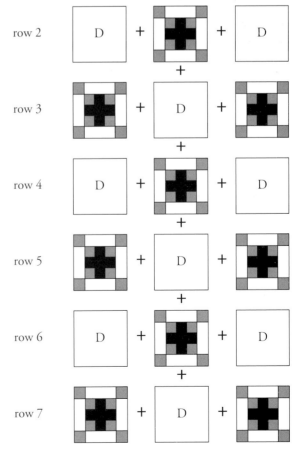

row 1

row 2

row 3

row 4

row 5

row 6

row 7

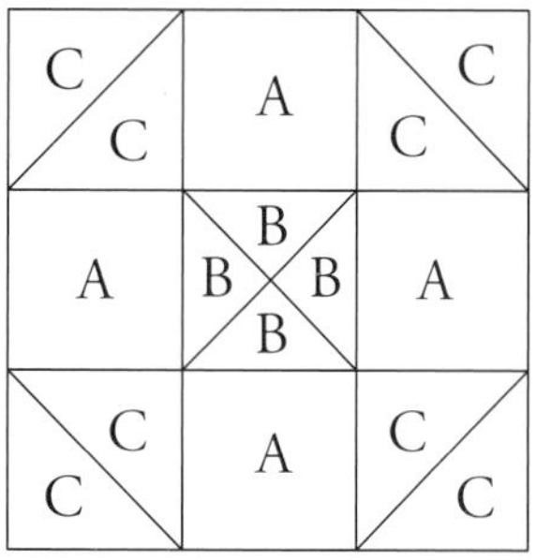

Cheers

Here is a simple-to-piece quilt that has lots of design possibilities. Don't let the simplicity fool you – this is a great block for color experimentation.

See photograph page 50.

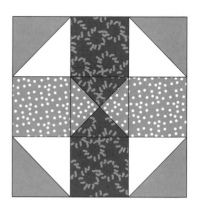

Fabric #1

Fabric #2

Fabric #3

Fabric #4

Yardage Chart					
	Wall	**Twin**	**Double**	**Queen**	**King**
	3 x 3	**4 x 7**	**5 x 7**	**6 x 8**	**7 x 8**
Fabric #					
1	1½	1½	1½	2	2¼
2	½	1½	1½	2	2¼
3	½	1	1¼	1¾	2
4	½.	1	1¼	1¾	2
Borders (finished sizes given)					
1st Border	1½" – ⅜	1½" – ½	1" – ½	2" – ⅞	2" – ⅞
2nd Border	4" – ⅞	2½" – ¾	3" – 1	4" – 1½	6" – 2
3rd Border	-	4" – 1⅛	5" – 1⅝	6" – 2	-
Batting	1½	6	6	6¼	9
Back	3	6	6⅛	8	9
Binding	¾	1	1	1	1¼
Finished Size	47" x 47"	64" x 100"	78" x 102"	84" x 108"	100" x 112"

Cutting the Strips					
Quilt	**Fabric #**	**Pattern Piece**	**Size of Strip**	**Number of Strips**	**Total Pieces Needed**
Wall	1	A	4½"	2	18
	1	B	3¾"	1	18
	2	A	4½"	2	18
	2	B	3¾"	1	18
	1st Border	-	2"	6	-
	2nd Border	-	4½"	6	-

| | | Cutting the Strips (continued) | | | |
Quilt	Fabric #	Pattern Piece	Size of Strip	Number of Strips	Total Pieces Needed
Twin	1	A	4½"	7	56
	1	B	3¾"	2	56
	2	A	4½"	7	56
	2	B	3¾"	2	56
	1st Border	-	2"	9	-
	2nd Border	-	3"	9	-
	3rd Border	-	4½"	9	-
Double	1	A	4½"	8	70
	1	B	3¾"	3	70
	2	A	4½"	8	70
	2	B	3¾"	3	70
	1st Border	-	1½"	10	-
	2nd Border	-	3½"	10	-
	3rd Border	-	5½"	10	-
Queen	1	A	4½"	11	96
	1	B	3¾"	3	96
	2	A	4½"	11	96
	2	B	3¾"	3	96
	1st Border	-	2½"	11	-
	2nd Border	-	4½"	11	-
	3rd Border	-	6½"	11	-
King	1	A	4½"	13	112
	1	B	3¾"	4	112
	2	A	4½"	13	112
	2	B	3¾"	4	112
	1st Border	-	2½"	12	-
	2nd Border	-	6½"	12	-

Note: C pieces are quick-pieced triangles, using fabric #3 and #4.

Cutting and Sewing the Pieces

Cut the strips indicated on the "Cutting the Strips" chart.

A Pieces. Divide the 4½" strips of fabrics #1 and #2 into squares.

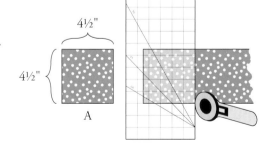

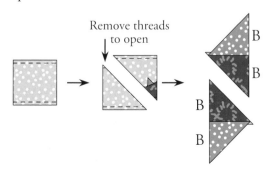

B Pieces. These are sandwich-pieced triangles (see "Rules to Cut By" page 10). Place opened 3¾" strips of fabrics #1 and #2 right sides together. Sew together on both long edges. Divide the strips into 3¾" squares, then slice the squares into triangles. Pull tips apart and press seams to one side.

29

"Chain Sew" (see page 12) these triangles together in pairs.

Open and press seams to one side. They should look like this:

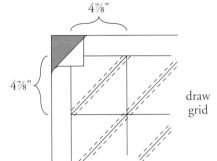

4⅞"

4⅞"

draw grid

C Pieces. These are made with quick-pieced triangles. See page 11 for drawing, sewing and cutting instructions. Use fabrics #3 and #4, and place them right sides together.

4½"

C

C

Refer to this chart for grid size and how many squares to draw.

Quilt Size	Wallhanging	Twin	Double	Queen	King
Grid Size	4⅞"	4⅞"	4⅞"	4⅞"	4⅞"
# of Squares across x down	6 x 3	8 x 7	7 x 10	6 x 12	8 x 14

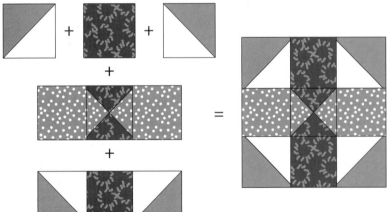

Assembling the Block

Sew block together using the diagram to the left.

Follow the "Sewing the Quilt Top Together" section on pages 14-15 to complete your quilt top.

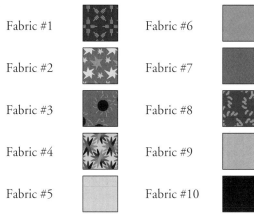

Fabric #1   Fabric #6

Fabric #2   Fabric #7

Fabric #3   Fabric #8

Fabric #4   Fabric #9

Fabric #5   Fabric #10

Fabric #11

Flying High

Kites and tails are taking off in every direction making a colorful display in this simple quilt pattern. We mixed and matched ten different fabrics for the kites, making each one unique. The kite tails are embroidered and appliquéd in the lattice strips, adding a touch of whimsy.

See photograph page 55.

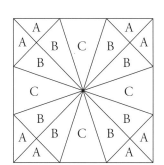

Yardage Chart					
	Wall **3 x 3**	**Twin** **3 x 5**	**Double** **4 x 5**	**Queen** **5 x 6**	**King** **6 x 7**
Fabric #					
1 to 10	⅓ each	½ each	⅝ each	⅞ each	⅞ each
11	⅞	1⅝	2	2½	3
Lattice Strips	⅞	1⅜	1⅞	2½	3⅜
Corner Blocks	⅓	⅓	⅜	½	⅝
OR, use scraps of fabrics #1 through #10					
Borders (finished sizes given)					
1st Border	1" – ⅓	1½" – ⅝	2½" – 1	5" – 1⅞	4" – 1⅝
2nd Border	4" – 1	3½" – 1⅛	4" – 1⅜	-	-
3rd Border	-	5" – 1⅝	6" – 2	-	-
Batting	3½	6	6⅛	6⅛	9
Back	3½	6	6⅛	8	9
Binding	1	1	1	1	1¼
Finished Size	58" x 58"	68" x 98"	78" x 103"	88" x 103"	97" x 112"
Bows on kite tails in the lattice are made from the leftover scraps of fabrics #1 to #10					

Quilt	Fabric	Pattern Piece	Size of Strip	Number of Strips	Total Pieces Needed
			Cutting the Strips		
Wall	#1 to #10	A	5¼"	1 each	72
	#1 to #10	B	3½"	1 each	72
	#11	C	7"	3	36
	Lattice	-	3½"	8	24
	Corner Blocks	-	3½"	2	16
	1st Border	-	1½"	6	-
	2nd Border	-	4½"	6	-
Twin	#1 to #10	A	5¼"	1 each	224
	#1 to #10	B	3½"	2 each	224
	#11	C	7"	7	112
	Lattice	-	3½"	14	42
	Corner Blocks	-	3½"	2	24
	1st Border	-	2"	9	-
	2nd Border	-	4"	9	-
	3rd Border	-	5½"	9	-
Double	#1 to #10	A	5¼"	1 each	280
	#1 to #10	B	3½"	3 each	280
	#11	C	7"	9	140
	Lattice	-	3½"	17	50
	Corner Blocks	-	3½"	3	30
	1st Border	-	3"	10	-
	2nd Border	-	4½"	10	-
	3rd Border	-	6½"	10	-
Queen	#1 to #10	A	5¼"	2 each	384
	#1 to #10	B	3½"	4 each	384
	#11	C	7"	12	192
	Lattice	-	3½"	24	72
	Corner Blocks	-	3½"	4	42
	Border	-	5½"	11	-
King	#1 to #10	A	5¼"	2 each	448
	#1 to #10	B	3½"	4 each	448
	#11	C	7"	14	224
	Lattice	-	3½"	33	98
	Corner Blocks	-	3½"	5	56
	Border	-	4½"	12	-

Cutting the Pieces

Cut the strips indicated on the "Cutting the Strips" chart.

A Pieces*. Divide the 5¼" strips of fabrics #1 to #10 into squares. Criss-cross slice them into triangles.

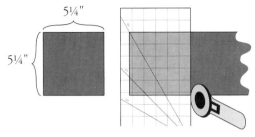

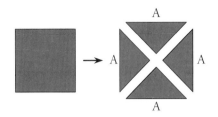

*Or use Companion Angle™. Cut strips 2½" wide.

B Pieces. Divide the folded 3½" strips of fabrics #1 to #10 into rectangles every 7".

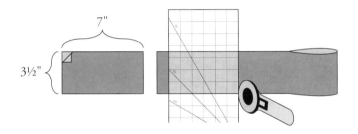

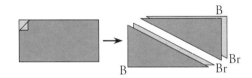

Slice them into triangles.

Be sure strips are folded when cutting rectangles as this will give you **B** and **Br** (**B** reverse) when you slice them.

C Pieces. Trace the **C** template onto the 7" strips of fabric #11 and slice on the lines.

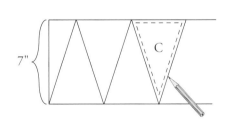

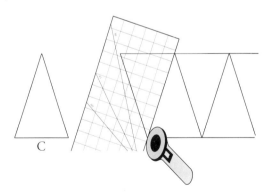

Assembling the Block

Sew your block together following the steps below. Be sure to mix up your fabrics #1 to #10 as you sew the **A**'s and **B**'s together, making lots of color combinations. Fabric #11, piece **C**, always stays the same.

a. Sew **A**'s together in pairs.

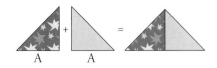

b. Sew **B**'s together in pairs.

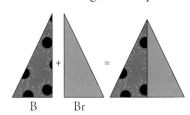

c. Sew **A** and **B** units together.

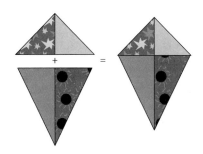

d. Sew a **C** piece onto the side of each kite, sewing to the same side each time.

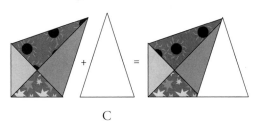

C

e. Lay the quarters on the floor or a table to mix up the colors the way you like. Sew quarters together in twos, then sew halves together to make blocks.

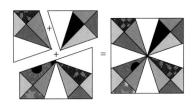

Constructing the Quilt Top

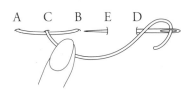

Use the stem stitch to embroider the kite tails onto your lattice strips. Appliqué the bows on using the instructions for appliqué in the Garden Gate pattern (pages 89-90).

A C B E D

Sew the lattice strips on and the blocks together as follows: (your number of blocks will vary depending on quilt size):

Stem Stitch Enlargement.

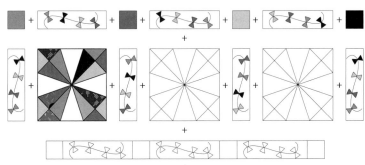

Follow the "Sewing the Quilt Top Together" section on pages 14-15 to complete your quilt top.

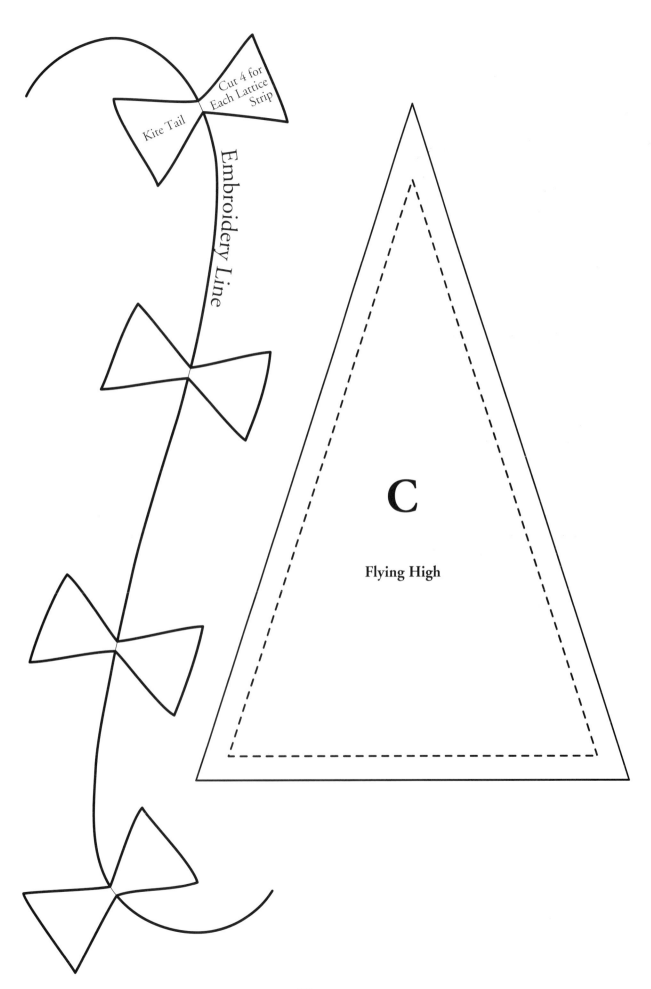

Cut 4 for
Each Lattice
Strip

Kite Tail

Embroidery Line

C

Flying High

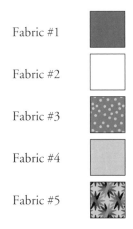

Harvest Star

This beginner block is a perfect setting to show off pretty florals or pictorial fabrics in the center. Easy to piece, this one is a good choice for everyone to try.

See photograph page 56.

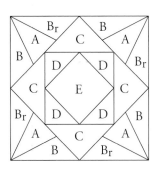

Fabric #1

Fabric #2

Fabric #3

Fabric #4

Fabric #5

Yardage Chart					
	Wall	**Twin**	**Double**	**Queen**	**King**
	3 x 3	**4 x 7**	**5 x 7**	**6 x 8**	**7 x 8**
Fabric #					
1	⅜	1	1⅛	1½	1¾
2	¾	2⅛	2⅝	3½	4
3	⅝	1⅛	1⅜	1⅞	2⅛
4	⅜	¾	⅞	1¼	1⅜
5	⅜	⅝	¾	1	1⅛
Borders (finished size given)					
1st Border	1" – ⅓	1½" – ½	1" – ½	2" – ⅞	2" – ⅞
2nd Border	4" – ⅞	2½" – ¾	3" – 1	4" – 1½	6" – 2
3rd Border	-	4" – 1⅛	5" – 1⅝	6" – 2	-
Batting	1½	6	6	6¼	9
Back	3	6	6⅛	8	9
Binding	¾	1	1	1	1¼
Finished Size	46" x 46'"	64" x 100"	78" x 102"	84" x 108"	100" x 112"

Cutting the Strips					
Quilt	Fabric #	Pattern Piece	Size of Strip	Number of Strips	Total Pieces Needed
Wall	1	A	5¼"	2	36
	2	B	2½"	9	72
	3	C	5⅛"	3	36
	4	D	3⅞"	3	36
	5	E	4¾"	2	9
	1st Border	-	1½"	6	-
	2nd Border	-	4½"	6	-
Twin	1	A	5¼"	6	112
	2	B	2½"	28	224
	3	C	5⅛"	7	112
	4	D	3⅞"	6	112
	5	E	4¾"	4	28
	1st Border	-	2"	9	-
	2nd Border	-	3"	9	-
	3rd Border	-	4½"	9	-
Double	1	A	5¼"	7	140
	2	B	2½"	35	280
	3	C	5⅛"	9	140
	4	D	3⅞"	7	140
	5	E	4¾"	5	35
	1st Border	-	1½"	10	-
	2nd Border	-	3½"	10	-
	3rd Border	-	5½"	10	-
Queen	1	A	5¼"	9	192
	2	B	2½"	48	384
	3	C	5⅛"	12	192
	4	D	3⅞"	10	192
	5	E	4¾"	6	48
	1st Border	-	2½"	11	-
	2nd Border	-	4½"	11	-
	3rd Border	-	6½"	11	-
King	1	A	5¼"	11	224
	2	B	2½"	56	448
	3	C	5⅛"	14	224
	4	D	3⅞"	12	224
	5	E	4¾"	7	56
	1st Border	-	2½"	12	-
	2nd Border	-	6½"	12	-

Cutting the Pieces

Cut the strips indicated on the "Cutting the Strips" chart.

A Pieces. Lay the **A** template on the 5¼" wide strips of fabric #1 and mark as shown. Note: The tips will hang slightly off the edge each time.

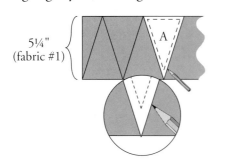

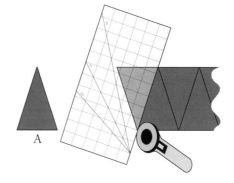

B Pieces. Lay the **B** template on the 2½" strips of fabric #2 and mark as shown. Again, the tip will hang slightly off the edge each time.

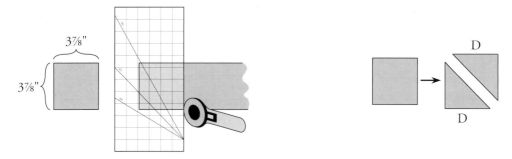

C Pieces. Divide the 5⅛" strips of fabric #3 into squares. Slice squares diagonally into triangles.

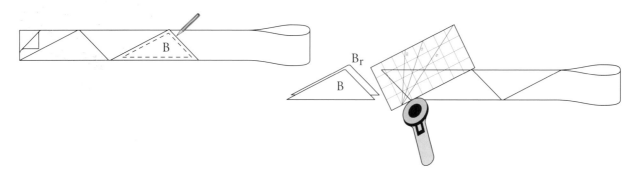

D Pieces. Divide the 3⅞" strips of fabric #4 into squares. Slice squares diagonally into triangles.

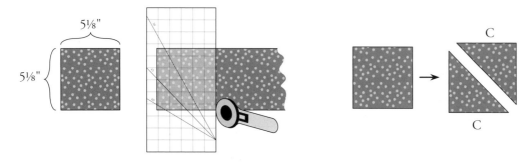

E Pieces. Divide the 4¾" strips of fabric #5 into squares.

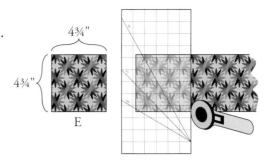

Assembling the Block

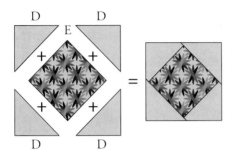

Sew **D**'s to **E** to make the center unit.

Sew **C**'s to the center unit. Set aside.

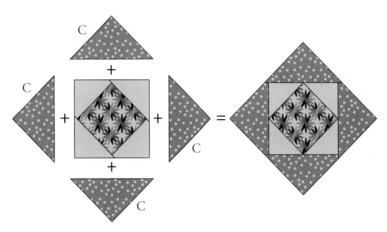

Construct the corners as shown below. Sew four **B/A/B** units together.

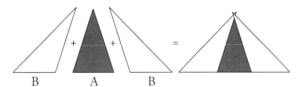

Sew the four **B/A/B** units to the large center unit to complete the block.

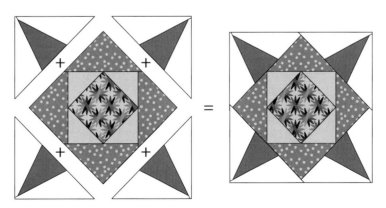

Follow the "Sewing the Quilt Top Together" section on pages 14-15 to complete your quilt top.

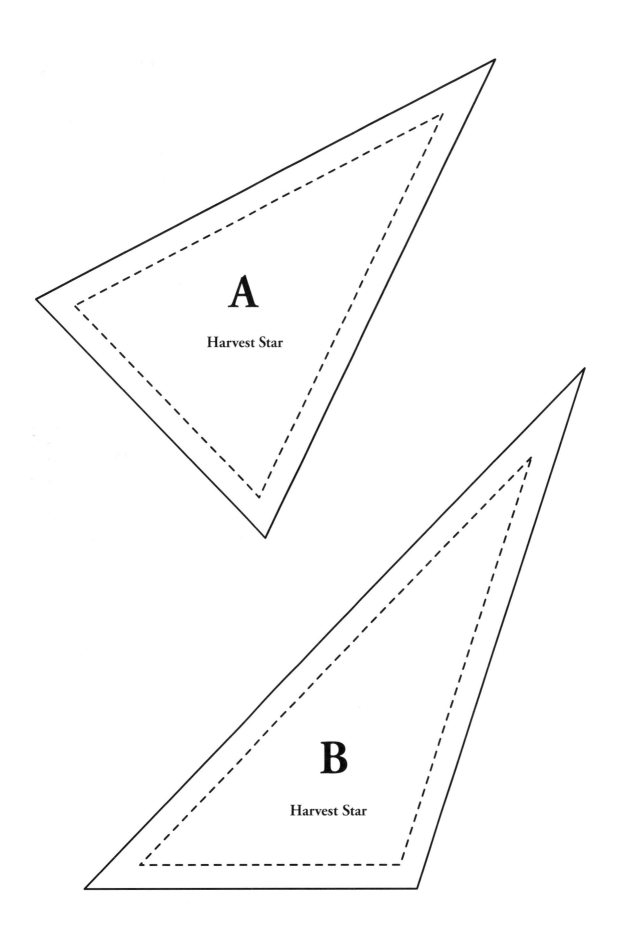

A

Harvest Star

B

Harvest Star

Lightening Strikes

This bold eye-catching design will please those who like a more modern flair. After making the blocks, experiment with turning them in different directions to create different looks. This pattern is best suited for someone with machine piecing experience.

See photograph page 61.

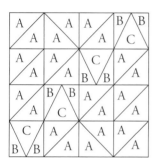

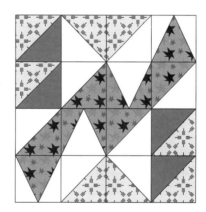

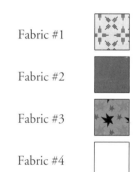

Fabric #1

Fabric #2

Fabric #3

Fabric #4

Yardage Chart					
	Wall 4 x 4	Twin 4 x 7	Double 6 x 8	Queen 6 x 8	King 8 x 8
Fabric #					
1	1	1¾	2¾	2¾	3
2	½	⅞	1⅜	1⅜	1½
3	1	1⅔	2¾	2¾	3⅝
4	1½	2½	4⅜	4⅜	5
Borders (finished sizes given)					
1st Border	1" – ⅓	1" – ½	3" – 1⅛	2" – ⅞	6" – 2⅜
2nd Border	2" – ½	3" – 1⅛	-	4" – 1½	-
3rd Border	4" – ⅞	5" – 1⅝	-	6" – 2⅛	-
Batting	3	6	6	6¼	9⅔
Back	3	6⅛	6⅛	8	9⅜
Binding	1	1	1	1	1¼
Finished Size	62" x 62"	66" x 102"	78" x 102"	84" x 108"	108" x 108"

		Cutting the Strips			
Quilt	Fabric #	Pattern Piece	Size of Strip	Number of Strips	Total Pieces Needed
Wall	3	B	4¼"	2	64
	3	C	3¾"	2	32
	4	B	4¼"	2	64
	4	C	3¾"	2	32
	1st Border	-	1½"	6	-
	2nd Border	-	2½"	6	-
	3rd Border	-	4½"	6	-
Twin	3	B	4¼"	3	112
	3	C	3¾"	4	56
	4	B	4¼"	3	112
	4	C	3¾"	4	56
	1st Border	-	1½"	9	-
	2nd Border	-	3½"	9	-
	3rd Border	-	5½"	9	-
Double	3	B	4¼"	6	192
	3	C	3¾"	6	96
	4	B	4¼"	6	192
	4	C	3¾"	6	96
	Border	-	3⅛"	10	-
Queen	3	B	4¼"	6	192
	3	C	3¾"	6	96
	4	B	4¼"	6	192
	4	C	3¾"	6	96
	1st Border	-	2½"	11	-
	2nd Border	-	4½"	11	-
	3rd Border	-	6½"	11	-
King	3	B	4¼"	8	256
	3	C	3¾"	10	128
	4	B	4¼"	8	256
	4	C	3¾"	10	128
	Border	-	6½"	12	-

Cutting and Sewing the Pieces

*or, use 3" finished SPEED GRIDS®

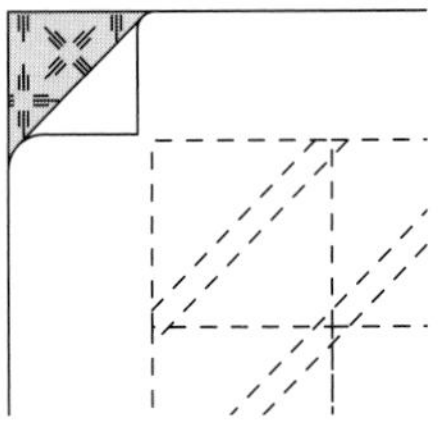

Cut the strips indicated on the "Cutting the Strips" chart.

A Pieces*. All **A** pieces are made from quick-pieced triangles. See page 11 of "Rules to Cut By" for drawing, sewing and cutting instructions. You will make three different sets of quick-pieced triangles for this quilt. Lay the following fabrics right sides together:

a. #1 and #2   b. #1 and #4   c. #3 and #4

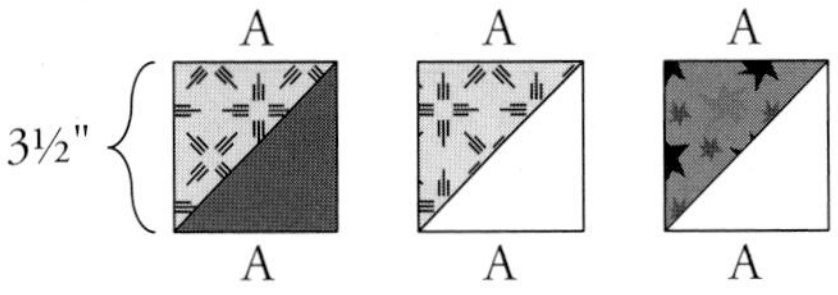

42

Refer to the chart below for drawing grids for each of the three combinations.

Quilt Size	Wall	Twin	Double	Queen	King
Grid Size	3⅞"	3⅞"	3⅞"	3⅞"	3⅞"
# of Squares across x down	8 x 4	8 x 7	8 x 12	8 x 12	10 x 13

B Pieces. Divide the 4¼" strips of fabrics #3 and #4 into rectangles every 2⅛".

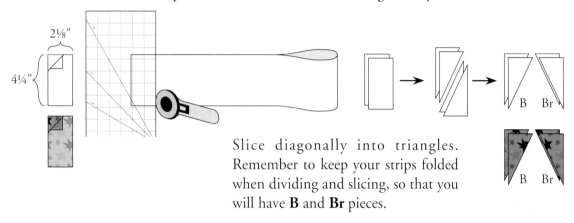

Slice diagonally into triangles. Remember to keep your strips folded when dividing and slicing, so that you will have **B** and **Br** pieces.

C Pieces. You will need your **C** template for this step. Lay the template on your 3¾" strips of fabrics #3 and #4, and draw as shown.

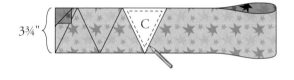

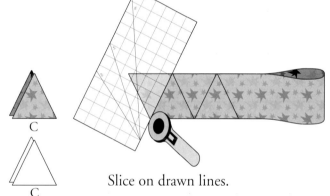

Slice on drawn lines.

Assembling the Block

Sew **B** and **C** pieces together as follows:

    a. Chain sew **B**'s on one side of **C**.

    b. Press and chain sew **Br**'s on the other side.

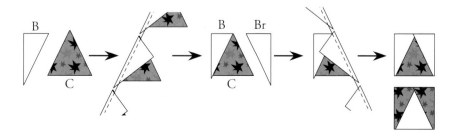

Construct the block in rows, watching fabric placement of **A** pieces to make the design.

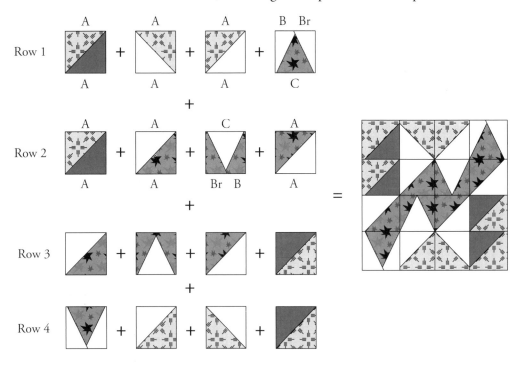

Follow the "Sewing the Quilt Top Together" section on pages 14-15 to complete your quilt top.

The quilt picture on page 61 was constructed by half-turning every other block.

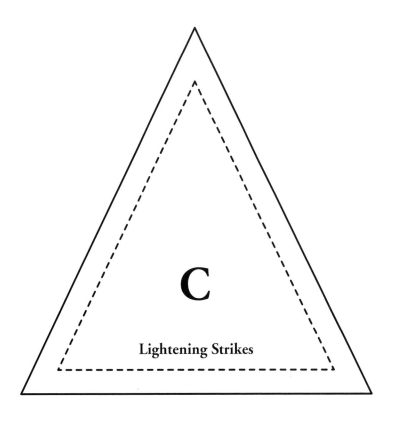

C

Lightening Strikes

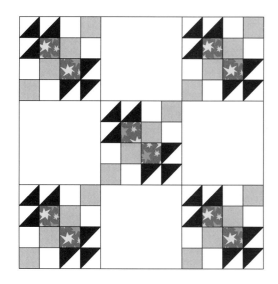

Bouillabaisse

We named this pattern "Bouillabaisse" (fish soup) because the pattern looks like fish swimming in all different directions. The construction of the quilt is not difficult, but there are lots of small pieces, so a beginner should keep this in mind. The end result is well worth the effort.

See photograph page 49.

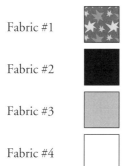

Fabric #1

Fabric #2

Fabric #3

Fabric #4

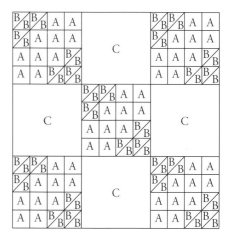

Yardage Chart					
	Wall or Lap **4 x 4**	**Twin** **4 x 7**	**Double** **6 x 8**	**Queen** **6 x 8**	**King** **8 x 8**
Fabric #					
1	⅓	½	⅞	⅞	1⅛
2	¾	1	2	2	2⅝
3	⅝	⅞	1⅝	1⅝	2
4	2⅓	3¼	6⅓	6⅓	8¼
Borders (finished sizes given)					
1st Border	1½" – ⅜	1" – ½	3" – 1⅛	2" – ⅞	6" – 2⅜
2nd Border	4" – ⅞	3" – 1⅛	-	4" – 1½	-
3rd Border	-	5" – 1⅜	-	6" – 2⅛	-
Batting	1¾	6⅛	6⅛	6¼	9⅜
Back	1⅞	6	6	8¼	9⅔
Binding	1	1	1	1	1¼
Finished Size	59" x 59"	66" x 102"	78" x 102"	84" x 108"	108" x 108"

			Cutting the Strips		
Quilt	Fabric #	Pattern Piece	Size of Strip	Number of Strips	Total Pieces Needed
Wall or Lap	1	A	1½"	6	160
	3	A	1½"	12	320
	4	A	1½"	12	320
	4	C	4½"	8	64
	1st Border	-	2"	6	-
	2nd Border	-	4½"	6	-
Twin	1	A	1½"	9	240
	3	A	1½"	18	480
	4	A	1½"	18	480
	4	C	4½"	11	96
	1st Border	-	1½"	9	-
	2nd Border	-	3½"	9	-
	3rd Border	-	5½"	9	-
Double	1	A	1½"	18	480
	3	A	1½"	35	960
	4	A	1½"	35	960
	4	C	4½"	22	192
	Border	-	3½"	10	-
Queen	1	A	1½"	18	480
	3	A	1½"	35	960
	4	A	1½"	35	960
	4	C	4½"	22	192
	1st Border	-	2½"	11	-
	2nd Border	-	4½"	11	-
	3rd Border	-	6½"	11	-
King	1	A	1½"	23	640
	3	A	1½"	46	1280
	4	A	1½"	46	1280
	4	C	4½"	29	256
	Border	-	6½"	12	-

Cutting and Sewing the Pieces

Cut the strips indicated on the "Cutting the Strips" chart.

A Pieces. Divide your 1½" strips of fabric #1 into squares.

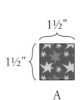

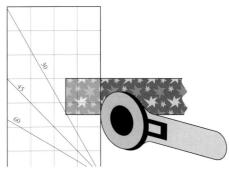

1½"

1½"

A

Strip your other 1½" strips of fabric #3 and #4 right sides together in pairs as shown.

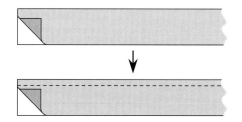

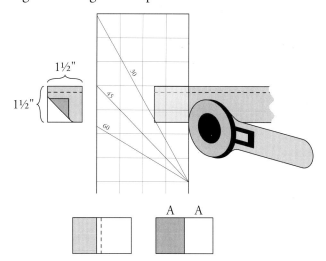

Cut into 1½" squares, before opening up.

Open and iron seams toward dark side.

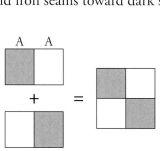

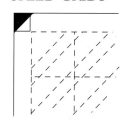

Sew these units together in pairs with colors opposite each other.

B Pieces*. These are all quick-pieced triangles. See page 11 of "Rules to Cut By" for drawing, sewing and cutting instructions. Refer to the chart below for square size and how many to draw. Use fabrics #2 and #4.

*or, use 1" finished SPEED GRIDS®

Quilt Size	Wall	Twin	Double	Queen	King
Grid Size	1⅞"	1⅞"	1⅞"	1⅞"	1⅞"
# of Squares across x down	20 x 12	20 x 18	20 x 36	20 x 36	20 x 48

C Pieces. Divide the 4½" strips of fabric #4 into squares.

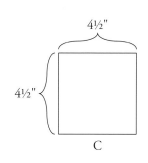

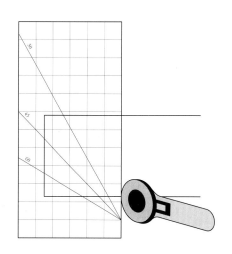

Assembling the Block

Sew your block together following the steps below.

Each block has five "fish" units assembled in this manner:

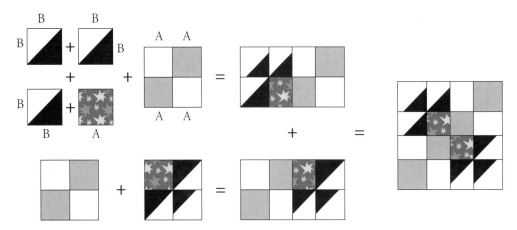

Sew these units to piece **C** in the following order:

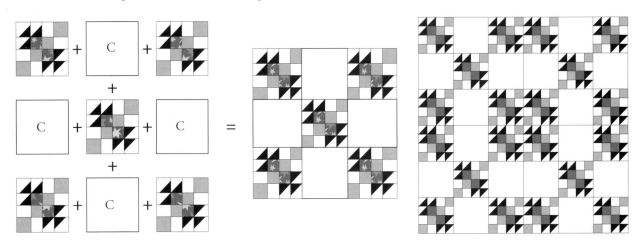

Follow the "Sewing the Quilt Top Together" section on pages 14–15 to complete your quilt top.

Variation: The blocks in this quilt as pictured on page 49 were turned a half turn. The quilt needs to have a even number of blocks and rows to make the design complete. Above right shows the pattern formed if the blocks are set side by side without a half turn. In this case, you would not necessarily need to make an even number of blocks.

Bouillabaise
59" x 59"

Rust and blue make a good color combination
for an intricate-looking but easy-to-piece quilt.

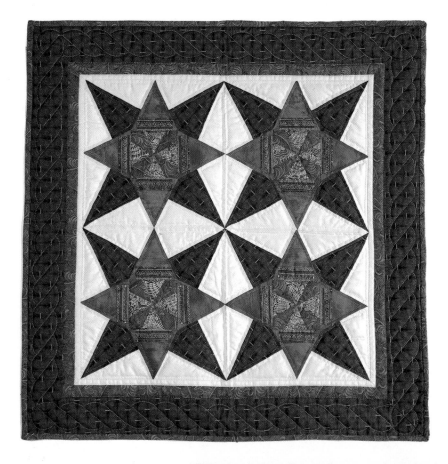

Blast Off!
33" x 33"

Rich tones of turquoise
and purple glow in this
unusual exploding star.

Cheers
47" x 47"

Beautiful fabrics are
shown off nicely
in a simple design.

Cross My Heart
47" x 47"

The shading of black, red and rose fabrics give
an almost transparent, stained-glass appearance.

Corn Chowder
44" x 56"

This quilt really looks like corn chowder!
The scrappy look in colonial colors is one of our favorites.

Corn Chowder
46" x 46"

Amish colors change the appearance of the design so dramatically from the quilt at the left, that one hardly recognizes it as the same design. The blue and black corners of the blocks form a secondary pattern as they come together.

Crossing Over
67" x 67"

Pretty blues and pinks form a simple chain quilt reminiscent of other traditional chain patterns.

Don Quixote's Dream
60" x 60"

Subtle shadings of red and rose against black provide
continuity for an abstract design. It takes a moment,
but suddenly you begin to see the small and large
black windmills scattered over the quilt.

Flying High
66" x 95"

Easy to piece, the trick here is to get all twelve points to match at the center of each block!

Harvest Star
66" x 89"

This design makes a nice showcase for outstanding prints such
as the cactus flowers used in the center of the blocks and as a border.

Spun Gold
44½" x 62"

The contrast between fabrics in this star-within-a-star is subtle,
and gives the feeling of sitting in a field of sunflowers on a cool, starry night.

Shining Through
31" x 31"

The center of this whimsical star is perfect for pictorial prints. The design is simple, but the angles are unusual enough to make it interesting.

Windy
42" x 42"

The Easy Eight™ tool makes those scary diamonds easy-as-pie in this simple little windblown quilt.

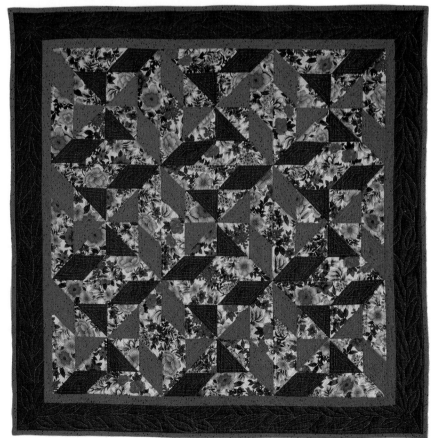

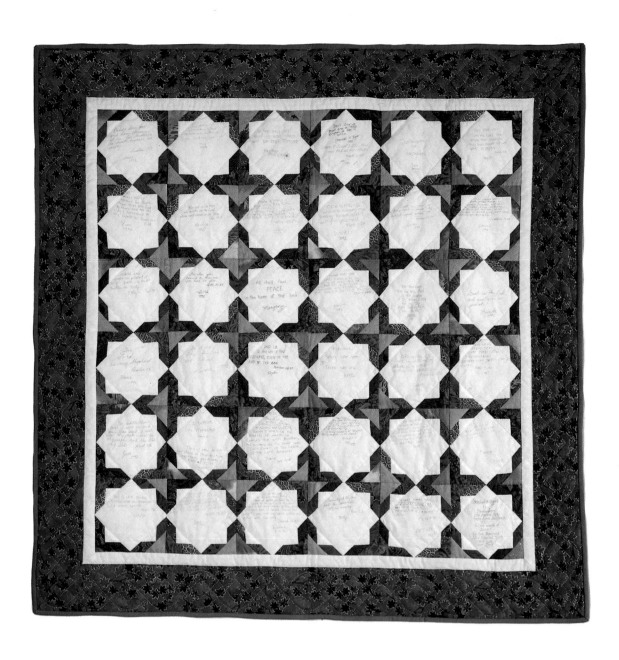

Star Chamber
44" x 44"

Jewel tones of blue and green sparkle between the white stars in this
special friendship quilt. Favorite scriptures and sentiments are "etched" in
cloth as a memory of what was happening at Piecemakers in the Spring of 1992!

Straight Arrow
44" x 55½"

Although this combination of cheerful primary prints produces
quite an active quilt, the blue and gold arrows stand out very nicely.

Straight Arrow
29" x 29"

A much more restful feeling
prevails here and a secondary
star pattern is formed by the
green triangles around the edge
of the quilt.

Lightening Strikes
60" x 60"

Definitely a
masculine design,
this quilt makes a
strong statement
as a wall quilt.
Pretty pinwheels
are also formed
when several
blocks are put
together.

Presidential Platform 1992
Jacket Front

Which direction is this block going? No one really knows and that is the fun of using a design that can be broken apart so many ways to design an article of clothing.

Presidential Platform 1992
Jacket Back

No Stress Threads Vest
Vest Front

What a way to use the small scraps you can't throw away! This vest is noticed wherever it goes and is also beautiful when made in soft or antique colors.

No Stress Threads Vest
Close-up detail of vest.

Garden Gate
47" x 59"

Looking through the lattice work into a bright and cheery flower
garden brings back memories of grandma's house. The use of 1930's
reproduction fabrics enhances the nostalgia of this pieced and appliquéd quilt.

Shining Through

This block is very effective when a pictorial print is used in the center. We chose a jungle print – the possibilities are endless! Here is an easy pattern, combining the use of strip piecing and templates.

See photograph page 58.

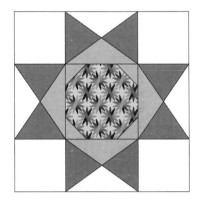

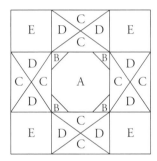

Fabric #1    Fabric #3

Fabric #2   Fabric #4

Yardage Chart						
	Small Wall **2 x 2**	**Wall** **3 x 3**	**Twin** **4 x 7**	**Double** **5 x 7**	**Queen** **6 x 8**	**King** **7 x 8**
Fabric #1	¼	⅜	¾	⅞	1	1⅜
Fabric #2	⅓	½	1⅛	1¼	1⅓	2
Fabric #3	¼	⅝	1⅓	1⅝	2⅛	2½
Fabric #4	½	⅞	1⅝	2½	3½	4⅛
Borders (finished sizes given)						
1st Border	1" – ¼	1" – ⅓	1½" – ½	1" – ½	2" – ⅞	2" – ⅞
2nd Border	3" – ½	4" – ⅞	2½" – ¾	3" – 1	4" – 1½	6" – 2
3rd Border	-	-	4" – 1⅛	5" – 1⅝	6" – 2	-
Batting	1	1½	6	6	6¼	9
Back	1	3	6	6⅛	8¼	9
Binding	¾	¾	1	1	1	1¼
Finished Size	32" x 32"	46" x 46"	64" x 100"	78" x 102"	84" x 108"	100" x 112"

Quilt	Fabric #	Pattern Piece	Size of Strip	Number of Strips	Total Pieces Needed
Small	1	A	5½"	1	4
Wall	2	B	3¼"	1	16
	2	C	2¼"	2	16
	3	D	3⅛"	2	32
	4	C	2¼"	2	16
	4	E	4"	2	16
	1st Border	-	1½"	4	-
	2nd Border	-	3½"	4	-
Wall	1	A	5½"	2	9
	2	B	3¼"	1	36
	2	C	2¼"	4	36
	3	D	3⅛"	5	72
	4	C	2¼"	4	36
	4	E	4"	4	36
	1st Border	-	1½"	6	-
	2nd Border	-	4½"	6	-
Twin	1	A	5½"	4	28
	2	B	3¼"	3	112
	2	C	2¼"	11	112
	3	D	3⅛"	14	224
	4	C	2¼"	11	112
	4	E	4"	12	112
	1st Border	-	2"	9	-
	2nd Border	-	3"	9	-
	3rd Border	-	4½"	9	-
Double	1	A	5½"	5	35
	2	B	3¼"	3	140
	2	C	2¼"	13	140
	3	D	3⅛"	17	280
	4	C	2¼"	13	140
	4	E	4"	14	140
	1st Border	-	1½"	10	-
	2nd Border	-	3½"	10	-
	3rd Border	-	5½"	10	-
Queen	1	A	5½"	7	48
	2	B	3¼"	4	192
	2	C	2¼"	18	192
	3	D	3⅛"	23	384
	4	C	2¼"	18	192
	4	E	4"	20	192
	1st Border	-	2½"	11	-
	2nd Border	-	4½"	11	-
	3rd Border	-	6½"	11	-

Cutting the Strips

		Cutting the Strips (continued)			
Quilt	Fabric #	Pattern Piece	Size of Strip	Number of Strips	Total Pieces Needed
King	1	A	5½"	8	56
	2	B	3¼"	5	224
	2	C	2¼"	21	224
	3	D	3⅛"	27	448
	4	C	2¼"	21	224
	4	E	4"	23	224
	1st Border	-	2½"	12	-
	2nd Border	-	6½"	12	-

Cutting the Pieces

Cut the strips indicated on the "Cutting the Strips" chart.

A Pieces. Divide the 5½" strips of fabric #1 into squares. Set aside.

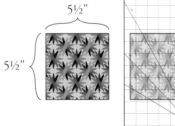
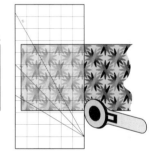

B Pieces. Divide the 3¼" strips of fabric #2 into squares.

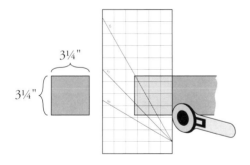

Criss-cross slice them into triangles.

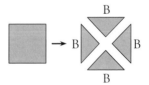

C Pieces. Lay your **C** template on the 2¼" strips of fabric #2 and #4 as shown, and trace. Slice on drawn lines.

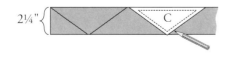
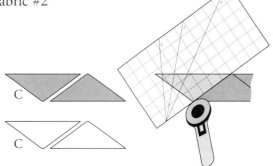

67

D Pieces. Lay your **D** template on the 3⅛" strip of fabric #3 as shown and trace. The tips on this one will hang off the edge slightly each time. Slice on drawn lines.

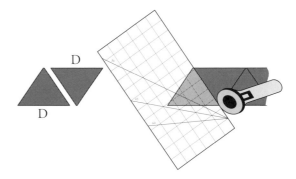

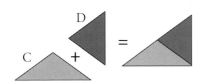

E Pieces. Divide the 4" strips of fabric #4 into squares.

Assembling the Blocks

Sew your block together following the steps below.

Sew all eight **C/D** units together.

Sew these units together in pairs. Set aside.

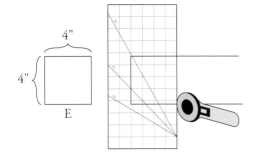

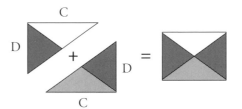

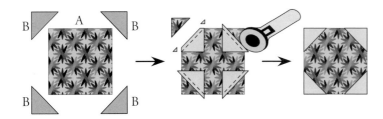

Sew the **B** corners onto the center **A** square as shown.

Cut off the underneath corners of fabric #1.

Complete the center row by sewing two **C/D/D/C** units to each side of the center piece **A/B/B/B/B**.

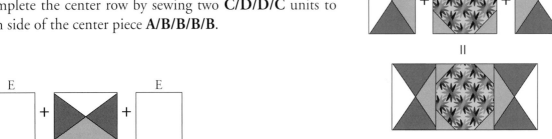

Make the top and bottom rows by sewing the **C/D/D/C** unit to the **E** corner pieces.

Sew the three rows together.

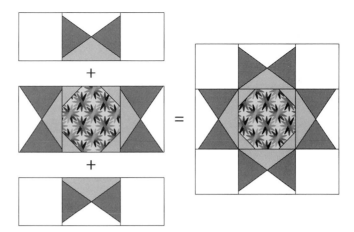

Follow the "Sewing the Quilt Top Together" section on pages 14-15 to complete your quilt top.

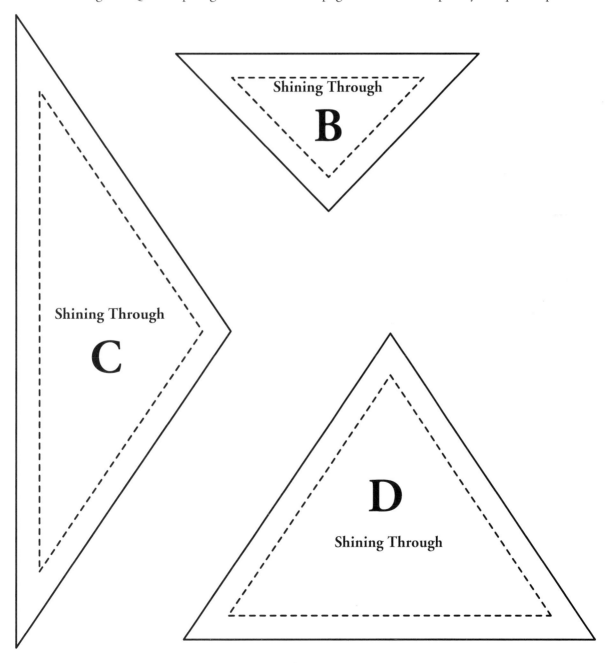

Don Quixote's Dream

This dynamic quilt has many patterns within patterns. Notice the design that the black areas make and all the different sized windmills. Don Quixote's Dream provides great opportunities for playing with color and we recommend it as an intermediate project.

See photograph page 54.

Fabric #1

Fabric #2

Fabric #3

Fabric #4

Fabric #5

Fabric #6

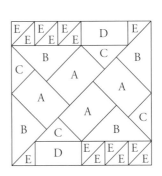

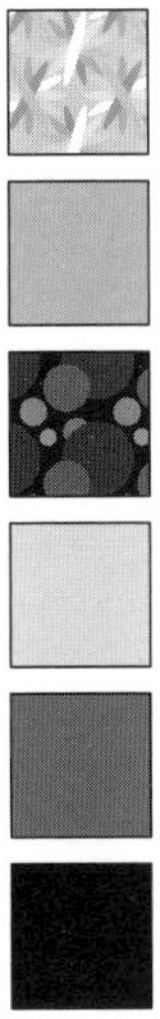

Yardage Chart					
	Wall **4 x 4**	**Twin** **4 x 7**	**Double** **5 x 7**	**Queen** **6 x 8**	**King** **7 x 8**
Fabric #					
1	⅝	⅞	1	1¼	1½
2	⅝	⅞	1	1¼	1½
3	½	¾	⅞	1	1¼
4	⅓	½	⅝	⅝	¾
5	¼	¼	⅓	½	½
6	⅞	1⅝	2	2¼	2⅝
Borders (finished sizes given)					
1st Border (background)	1" – ⅓	1½" – ½	1" – ½	2" – ⅞	2" – ⅞
2nd Border	2" – ⅝	2½" – ¾	3" – 1	4" – 1½	6" – 2
3rd Border	4" – 1	4" – 1⅛	5" – 1⅝	6" – 2	-
Batting	4	6	6	6¼	9
Back	4	6	6⅛	8	9
Binding	1	1	1	1	1¼
Finished Size	62" x 62"	64" x 100"	78" x 102"	84" x 108"	100" x 112"

					Cutting the Strips					
Quilt	Fabric #	Pattern Piece	Size of Strip	Number of Strips	Total Pieces Needed
Wall	1	A	4¾"	3	32
	2	A	4¾"	3	32
	3	B	5⅛"	2	32
	4	C	5¼"	1	32
	5	E	2⅞"	2	32
	6	B	5⅛"	2	32
	6	C	5¼"	1	32
	6	D	4½"	2	32
	1st Border	-	1½"	6	-
	2nd Border	-	2½"	6	-
	3rd Border	-	4½"	6	-
Twin	1	A	4¾"	5	56
	2	A	4¾"	5	56
	3	B	5⅛"	4	56
	4	C	5¼"	2	56
	5	E	2⅞"	2	56
	6	B	5⅛"	4	56
	6	C	5¼"	2	56
	6	D	4½"	4	56
	1st Border	-	2"	9	-
	2nd Border	-	3"	9	-
	3rd Border	-	4½"	9	-
Double	1	A	4¾"	6	70
	2	A	4¾"	6	70
	3	B	5⅛"	5	70
	4	C	5¼"	3	70
	5	E	2⅞"	3	70
	6	B	5⅛"	5	70
	6	C	5¼"	3	70
	6	D	4½"	5	70
	1st Border	-	1½"	10	-
	2nd Border	-	3½"	10	-
	3rd Border	-	5½"	10	-
Queen	1	A	4¾"	8	96
	2	A	4¾"	8	96
	3	B	5⅛"	6	96
	4	C	5¼"	3	96
	5	E	2⅞"	4	96
	6	B	5⅛"	6	96
	6	C	5¼"	3	96
	6	D	4½"	6	96
	1st Border	-	2½"	11	-
	2nd Border	-	4½"	11	-
	3rd Border	-	6½"	11	-

Cutting the Strips (continued)					
Quilt	Fabric #	Pattern Piece	Size of Strip	Number of Strips	Total Pieces Needed
King	1	A	4¾"	10	112
	2	A	4¾"	10	112
	3	B	5⅛"	7	112
	4	C	5¼"	4	112
	5	E	2⅞"	4	112
	6	B	5⅛"	7	112
	6	C	5¼"	4	112
	6	D	4½"	7	112
	1st Border	-	2½"	12	-
	2nd Border	-	6½"	12	-

Cutting and Sewing the Pieces

Cut the strips indicated on the "Cutting the Strips" chart.

A Pieces. Divide the 4¾" strips of fabrics #1 and #2 into rectangles every 3⅜".

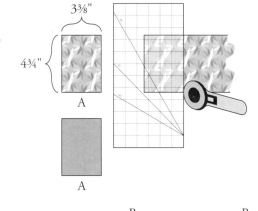

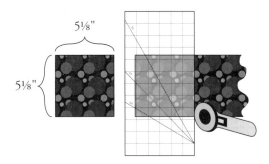

B Pieces*. Divide the 5⅛" strips of fabrics #3 and #6 into squares. Slice diagonally into triangles.

*or, use Easy Angle II™. Cut strips 4¾" wide.

C Pieces*. Divide the 5¼" strips of fabrics #4 and #6 into squares. Criss-cross slice into triangles.

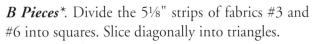

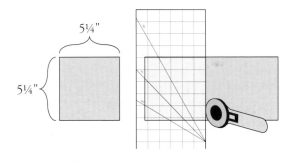

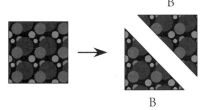

*or, use Companion Angle™. Cut strips 2½" wide.

D Pieces. Divide the 4½" strips of fabric #6 into rectangles every 2½".

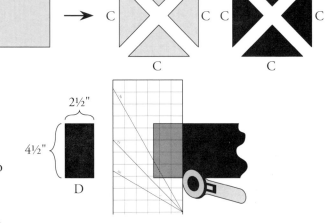

72

E Pieces. Most of the **E** pieces are quick-pieced triangles, except for the two single pieces in each block.

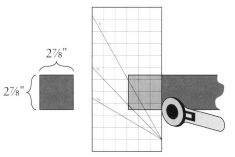

Single E's*. Divide the 2⅞" strips of fabric 5 into squares. Slice diagonally into triangles.

*or, use Easy Angle™. Cut strips 2½" wide.

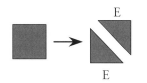

Quick-Pieced Triangles*. You will be making three sets of grids. See page 11 of "Rules to Cut By" for drawing, sewing and cutting instructions.

*or, use 2" SPEED GRIDS®.

Lay the following fabrics right sides together: fabrics #4 and #6; fabrics #2 and #6; fabrics #5 and #6. Use the chart below for drawing grids.

2½"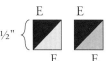

Quilt Size	Wall	Twin	Double	Queen	King
Grid Size	2⅞"	2⅞"	2⅞"	2⅞"	2⅞"
# of Squares across x down	3 x 3	7 x 4	7 x 5	8 x 6	8 x 7

Assembling the Block

Sew your block together following these steps:

1. Sew quick-pieced **E** triangles to **D** and **E**. Make 2 of these. Set aside.

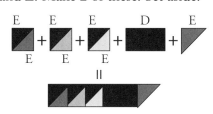

2. Sew both **B/A/C** units together. Make two of each kind.

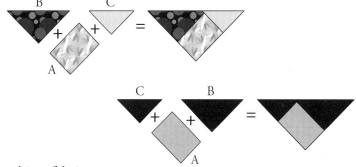

3. Piece **B/A/C** units together in two's, watching fabric placement in design. Add **E/E/E/D/E** unit.

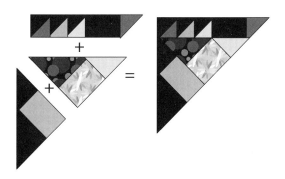

4. Sew two of these units together.

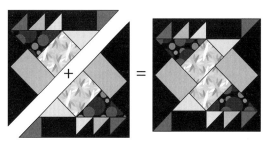

Follow the "Sewing the Quilt Top Together" section on pages 14-15 to complete your quilt top.

Straight Arrow

This eye-catching design makes a very appealing quilt with a kaleidoscope of fabrics and colors. This is an especially nice pattern for a man, but can easily be made feminine with your fabric choices. Straight Arrow is a nice challenge for someone with piecing experience.

See Photograph page 60.

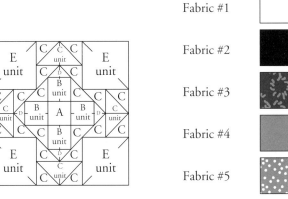

Fabric #1
Fabric #2
Fabric #3
Fabric #4
Fabric #5

Yardage Chart						
	Small Wall **2 x 2**	**Wall** **3 x 3**	**Twin** **4 x 7**	**Double** **5 x 7**	**Queen** **6 x 8**	**King** **7 x 8**
Fabric #						
1	⅓	⅜	⅞	1⅛	1⅓	1⅔
2	⅛	⅓.	¾	⅞	1⅛	1⅓.
3	⅛	⅓	¾	⅞	1⅛	1⅓
4	⅛	¼	⅜	½	⅔	¾
Borders (finished sizes given)						
1st Border	¼" – ⅛	1" – ⅓	1½" – ½	1" – ½	2" – ⅞	2" – ⅞
2nd Border	3" – ½	4" – ⅞	2½" – ¾	3" – 1	4" – 1½	6" – 2
3rd Border	-	-	4" – 1⅛	5" – 1⅝	6" – 2	-
Batting	1	1½	6	6	6¼	9
Back	1	3	6	6⅛	8	9
Binding	¾	¾	1	1	1	1¼
Finished Size	30" x 30"	46" x 46"	64" x 100"	78" x 102"	84" x 108"	100" x 112"

Quilt	Fabric #	Pattern Piece	Size of Strip	Number of Strips	Total Pieces Needed
		Cutting the Strips			
Small Wall	1	A	2½"	1	4
	1	C	2⅞"	2	32
	2	B	1½"	1	16
	2	D	1⅞"	1	16
	3	B	1½"	1	16
	3	D	1⅞"	1	16
	4	C	2⅞"	1	16
	1st Border	-	¾"	4	-
	2nd Border	-	3½"	4	-
Wall	1	A	2½"	1	9
	1	C	2⅞"	3	72
	2	B	1½"	3	36
	2	D	1⅞"	2	36
	3	B	1½"	3	36
	3	D	1⅞"	2	36
	4	C	2⅞"	2	36
	1st Border	-	1½"	6	-
	2nd Border	-	4½"	6	-
Twin	1	A	2½"	2	28
	1	C	2⅞"	8	224
	2	B	1½"	7	112
	2	D	1⅞"	6	112
	3	B	1½"	7	112
	3	D	1⅞"	6	112
	4	C	2⅞"	4	112
	1st Border	-	2"	9	-
	2nd Border	-	3"	9	-
	3rd Border	-	4½"	9	-
Double	1	A	2½"	3	35
	1	C	2⅞"	10	280
	2	B	1½"	9	140
	2	D	1⅞"	7	140
	3	B	1½"	9	140
	3	D	1⅞"	7	140
	4	C	2⅞"	5	140
	1st Border	-	1½"	10	-
	2nd Border	-	3½"	10	-
	3rd Border	-	5½"	10	-

| Cutting the Strips (continued) | | | | | |
Quilt	Fabric #	Pattern Piece	Size of Strip	Number of Strips	Total Pieces Needed
Queen	1	A	2½"	3	48
	1	C	2⅞"	14	384
	2	B	1½"	12	192
	2	D	1⅞"	9	192
	3	B	1½"	12	192
	3	D	1⅞"	9	192
	4	C	2⅞"	7	192
	1st Border	-	2½"	11	-
	2nd Border	-	4½"	11	-
	3rd Border	-	6½"	11	-
King	1	A	2½"	4	56
	1	C	2⅞"	16	448
	2	B	1½"	14	224
	2	D	1⅞"	11	224
	3	B	1½"	14	224
	3	D	1⅞"	11	224
	4	C	2⅞"	8	224
	1st Border	-	2½"	12	-
	2nd Border	-	6½"	12	-

Cutting and Sewing the Pieces

Cut the strips indicated on the "Cutting the Strips" chart.

A Pieces. Divide the 2½" strips of fabric #1 into squares.

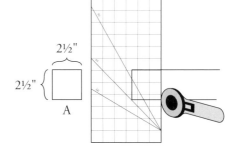

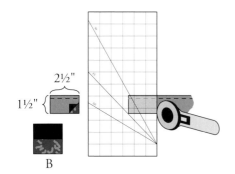

B Pieces. Take the 1½" strips of fabric #2 and #3 and sew them right sides together lengthwise. Slice this unit every 2½".

Open and press seams to one side. This unit is **B**.

C Pieces. Individual **C** pieces.

Divide the 2⅞" strips of fabrics #1 and #4 into squares.

Slice diagonally into triangles.

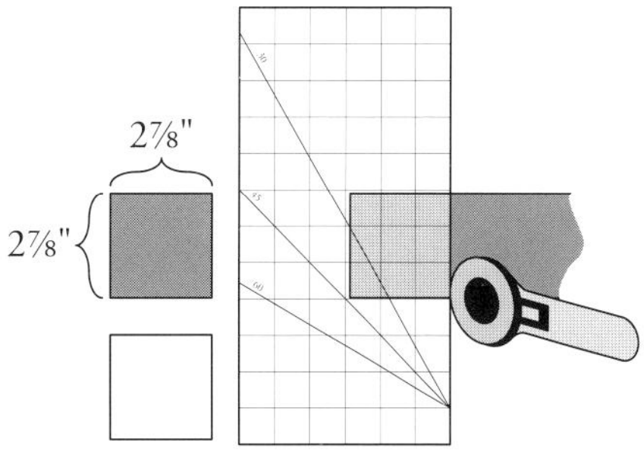
2⅞"
2⅞"

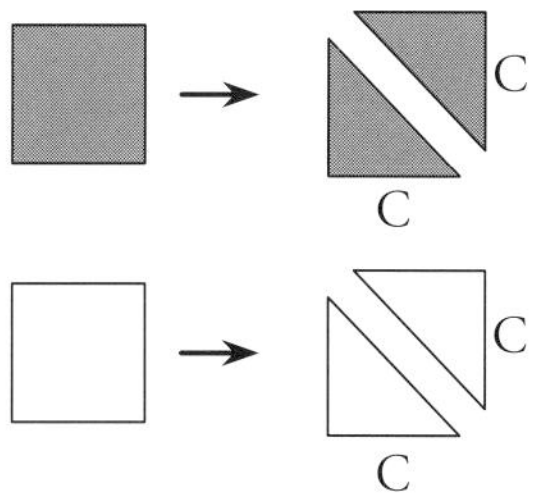
C
C
C
C

More C Pieces. Quick-pieced triangles* – see page 11 of "Rules to Cut By" for drawing, sewing and cutting instructions. Refer to the chart below to draw the grids. You will make 2 grids, one with fabrics #2 and #5 and the other with fabrics #3 and #5. The squares are drawn 2⅞".

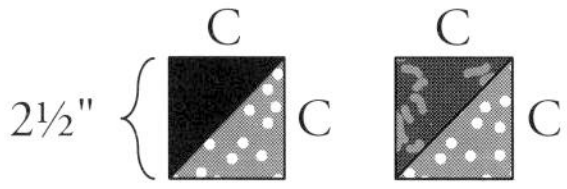
C
C
2½"
C
C

*or, use 2" finished SPEED GRIDS

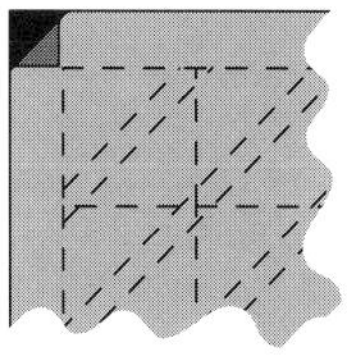

Quilt Size	Small Wall	Wall	Twin	Double	Queen	King
Grid Size	2⅞"	2⅞"	2⅞"	2⅞"	2⅞"	2⅞"
# of Squares across x down	3 x 3	6 x 3	8 x 7	10 x 7	12 x 8	14 x 8

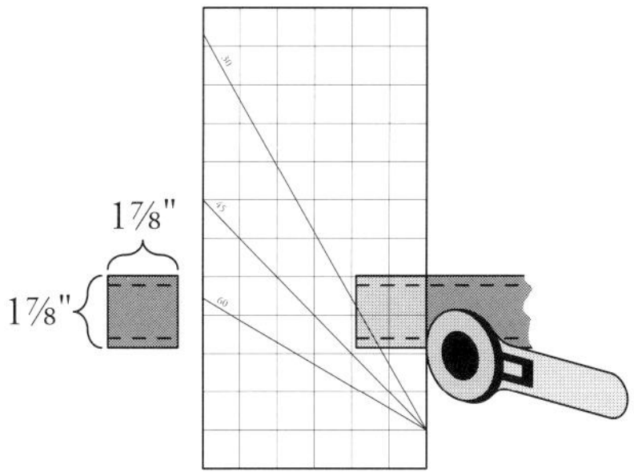
1⅞"
1⅞"

Unit D.

You will use sandwich-pieced triangles to sew these units together quickly. Sew your 1⅞" strips of fabrics #2 and #3 right sides together lengthwise on both long edges.

Divide into squares. Slice diagonally into triangles.

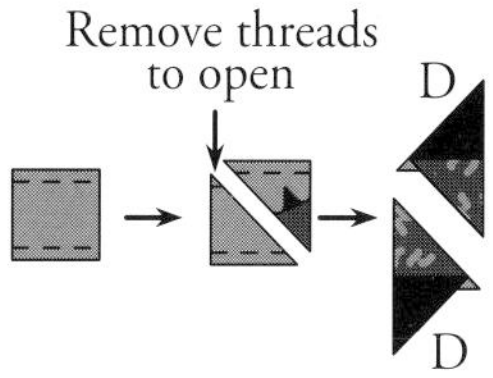
Remove threads to open
D
D

Unit E.

This is made with quick-pieced triangles. Refer to the chart below to draw your grid. Use fabrics #4 and #5. The squares are drawn 4⅞".

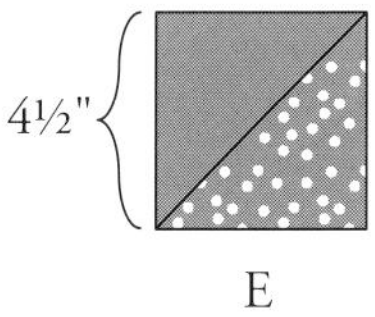
4½"
E

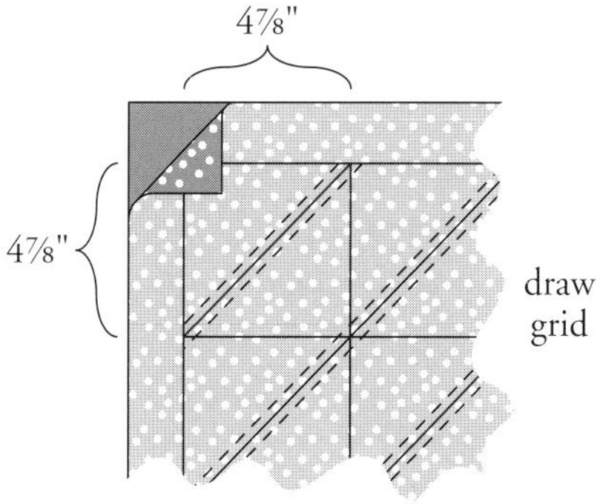
4⅞"
4⅞"
draw grid

Quilt Size	Small Wall	Wall	Twin	Double	Queen	King
Grid Size	4⅞"	4⅞"	4⅞"	4⅞"	4⅞"	4⅞"
# of Squares across x down	3 x 3	6 x 3	8 x 7	7 x 10	8 x 12	8 x 14

Assemble your block using the following steps.

Sew two **C/B/C** units for the center area. Add **D** to the top.

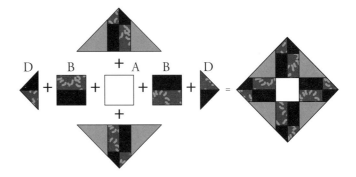

Sew the center following the diagram at the right. Sew top and bottom triangles to the center as shown. Set aside.

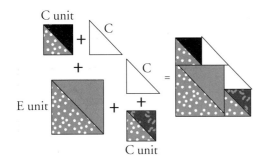

Sew the four corner units following the diagram at the left. Sew **C** units to individual **C** pieces. Notice the direction the pieces are turned for each side of the corner.

Sew these units onto **E**.

Attach each corner unit to the block center.

Follow the "Sewing the Quilt Top Together" section on pages 14-15 to complete your quilt top.

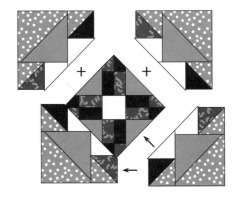

Corn Chowder

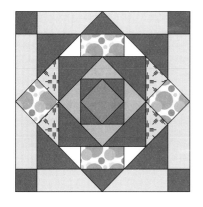

This pattern is a great example of how simple triangles and squares can make very pretty designs. When this quilt is put together, it has a wonderful "down home" feel. We have made two quilts – a traditional version done in Amish colors (which is specified in your charts) and a scrap version. We included the scrap quilt to show you how scraps can give you a totally different look. If you do the scrap quilt, just randomly cut the number of strips needed, watching dark and light areas.

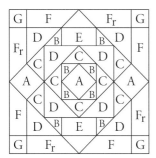

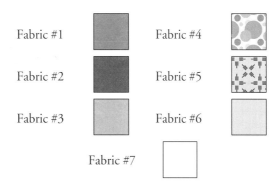

See photographs page 52 and 53.

Yardage Chart					
	Wall **3 x 3**	**Twin** **4 x 7**	**Double** **5 x 7**	**Queen** **6 x 8**	**King** **7 x 8**
Fabric #					
1	⅛	¼	⅓	⅓	⅜
2	⅞	2¼	2⅝	3⅝	4⅛
3	¼	½	½	¾	⅞
4	⅓	¾	⅞	1⅛	1¼
5	¼	½	½	¾	⅞
6	⅝	1⅜	1⅔	2¼	2⅝
7	¼	⅓	⅜	½	⅝
Borders (finished sizes given)					
1st Border	1" – ⅓	1½" – ½	1" – ½"	2" – ⅞	2" – ⅞
2nd Border	4" – ⅞	2½"– ¾	3" – 1	4" – ½	6" – 2
3rd Border	-	4"– 1⅛	5" – 1⅝	6" – 2	-
Batting	1½	6	6	6¼	9
Back	3	6	6⅛	8	9
Binding	¾	1	1	1	1¼
Finished Size	46" x 46"	64" x 100"	78" x 102"	84" x 108"	100" x 112"

Cutting the Strips

Quilt	Fabric #	Pattern Piece	Size of Strip	Number of Strips	Total Pieces Needed
Wall	1	A	2⅝"	1	9
	2	B	2⅜"	2	36
	2	C	3"	1	18
	2	D	3⅞"	4	72
	2	G	2"	2	36
	3	C	3"	2	36
	4	A	2⅝"	2	18
	4	E	3½"	1	18
	5	C	3"	2	36
	6	F	2"	8	72
	7	B	2⅜"	2	36
	1st Border	-	1½"	6	-
	2nd Border	-	4½"	6	-
Twin	1	A	2⅝"	2	28
	2	B	2⅜"	4	112
	2	C	3"	2	56
	2	D	3⅞"	12	224
	2	G	2"	6	112
	3	C	3"	4	112
	4	A	2⅝"	4	56
	4	E	3½"	3	56
	5	C	3"	4	112
	6	F	2"	23	224
	7	B	2⅜"	4	112
	1st Border	-	2"	9	-
	2nd Border	-	3"	9	-
	3rd Border	-	4½"	9	-
Double	1	A	2⅝"	3	35
	2	B	2⅜"	5	140
	2	C	3"	3	70
	2	D	3⅞"	14	280
	2	G	2"	7	140
	3	C	3"	5	140
	4	A	2⅝"	5	70
	4	E	3½"	4	70
	5	C	3"	5	140
	6	F	2"	28	280
	7	B	2⅜"	5	140
	1st Border	-	1½"	10	-
	2nd Border	-	3½"	10	-
	3rd Border	-	5½"	10	-

Cutting the Strips (continued)					
Quilt	Fabric #	Pattern Piece	Size of Strip	Number of Strips	Total Pieces Needed
Queen	1	A	2⅝"	3	48
	2	B	2⅜"	6	192
	2	C	3"	4	96
	2	D	3⅞"	20	384
	2	G	2"	10	192
	3	C	3"	7	192
	4	A	2⅝"	6	96
	4	E	3½"	5	96
	5	C	3"	7	192
	6	F	2"	39	384
	7	B	2⅜"	6	192
	1st Border	-	2½"	11	-
	2nd Border	-	4½"	11	-
	3rd Border	-	6½"	11	-
King	1	A	2⅝"	4	56
	2	B	2⅜"	7	224
	2	C	3"	4	112
	2	D	3⅞"	23	448
	2	G	2"	11	224
	3	C	3"	8	224
	4	A	2⅝"	7	112
	4	E	3½"	6	112
	5	C	3"	8	224
	6	F	2"	45	448
	7	B	2⅜"	7	224
	1st Border	-	2½"	12	-
	2nd Border	-	6½"	12	-

Cutting the Pieces

Cut the strips indicated on the "Cutting the Strips" chart.

A Pieces. Divide the 2⅝" strips of fabric #1 and #4 into squares.

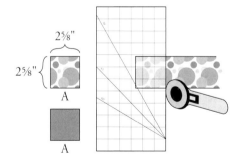

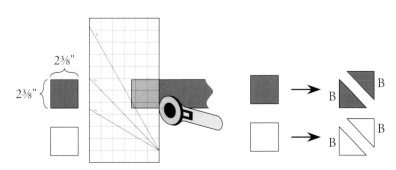

B Pieces*. Divide the 2⅜" strips of fabrics #2 and #7 into squares. Slice diagonally into triangles.

*or, use Easy Angle™. Cut the strips 2" wide.

C Pieces. Divide the 3" strips of fabric #2, #3 and #5 into squares.

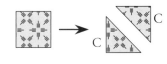

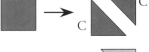

Slice into triangles.

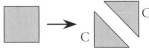

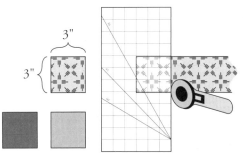

D Pieces*. Divide the 3⅞" strips of fabric #2 into squares.

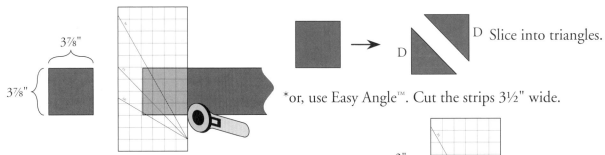

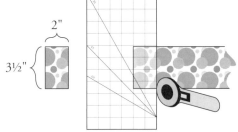

D Slice into triangles.

*or, use Easy Angle™. Cut the strips 3½" wide.

E Pieces. Divide the 3½" strips of fabric #4 into rectangles every 2".

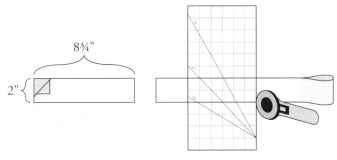

F Pieces. Divide the folded 2" strips of fabric #6 into rectangles every 8¾".

Be sure you have the strip folded so you will get **F** and **Fr** pieces.

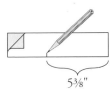

Measure along bottom edge of the rectangle and put a dot 5⅜" from the right edge. Lay the 45° line of your ruler along the bottom edge of the strip with the cutting edge at the dot, and slice. Make sure to lay the ruler in the direction shown. Leftovers of strips can be opened and laid right sides together to get four more pieces.

G Pieces. Divide the 2" strips of fabric #3 into squares.

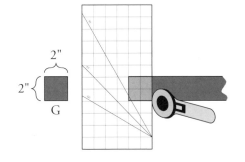

Assembling the Block

1. Sew **B** pieces to **A** to form the center unit.

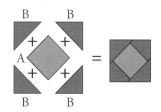

2. Sew **C** pieces to center unit.

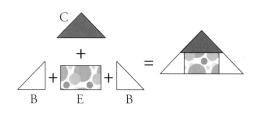

3. Sew **D** pieces onto this unit.

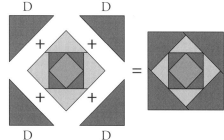

4. **B/E/B/C** units go together as pictured. Make two of these.

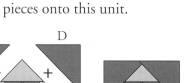

5. Make two **C/A/C** units.

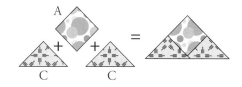

6. Sew the two **B/E/B/C** units on the top and bottom of the center and the two **C/A/C** units on the sides.

7. Sew the four **G/F** pieces. Be careful not to use the **Fr** pieces.

7.1. Sew the **Fr/D** units.

7.2. Sew the **G/F** and **Fr/D** units together to form the corners.

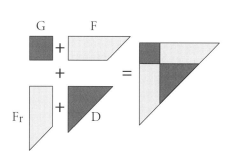

8. Sew these corners onto the block to finish.

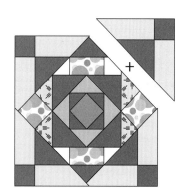

Follow the "Sewing the Quilt Top Together" section on pages 14-15 to complete your quilt top.

Garden Gate

Hand-appliquéd tulips peeking through the lattice bring this springtime quilt alive. Old-fashioned calico triangles spattered around the lattice make this pattern flow with color and charm. This one isn't difficult, but it does have a lot of small pieces, which makes it time consuming. We feel the end result is well worth the effort.

See photograph page 64.

Fabric #1

Fabric #2

Fabric #3

Fabrics #4 - 17

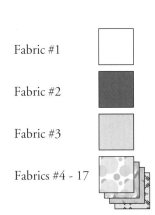

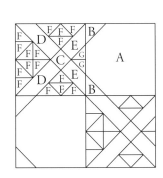

Yardage Chart					
	Wall	**Twin**	**Double**	**Queen**	**King**
	3 x 4	**4 x 7**	**5 x 7**	**6 x 8**	**7 x 8**
Fabric #					
1	⅞	2	2⅓	3	3⅝
2	1⅜	2¾	3½	4⅛	5⅜
3	⅛	¾	¾	⅓	⅓
4 to 17	¼ yd. each	⅓ yd. each	½ yd. each	½ yd. each	½ yd. each
Borders (finished sizes given)					
1st Border	¾" – ¼	1½ " – ½	1" – ½	2" – ⅞	2" – ⅞
2nd Border	1½" – ⅜	2½" – ¾	3" – 1	4" – 1½	6" – 2
3rd Border	4" – ⅞	4" – 1⅛	5" – 1⅝	6" – 2	-
Batting	1½	6	6	6¾	9
Back	3	6	6⅛	8	9
Binding	¾	1	1	1	1¼
Finished Size	48½" x 60½"	64" x 100"	78" x 102"	84" x 108"	100" x 112"

Cutting the Strips Chart					
Quilt	Fabric #	Pattern Piece	Size of Strip	Number of Strips	Total Pieces Needed
Wall	1	A	6½"	4	24
	2	B	2⅝"	2	48
	2	D	1¾"	6	48
	2	E	1¾"	4	48
	2	Leaf 1	template	-	48
	2	Leaf 2	template	-	24
	2	Leaf 3	template	-	24
	3	C	1¾"	1	24
	4 to 17	F	2⅜"	1 each	384
	4 to 17	G	2⅛"	1 each	24
	4 to 17	Tulip	template	-	72
	1st Border	-	1¼"	6	-
	2nd Border	-	2"	6	-
	3rd Border	-	4½"	6	-
Twin	1	A	6½"	10	56
	2	B	2⅝"	4	112
	2	D	1¾"	14	112
	2	E	1¾"	10	112
	2	Leaf 1	template	-	112
	2	Leaf 2	template	-	56
	2	Leaf 3	template	-	56
	3	C	1¾"	3	56
	4 to 17	F	2⅜"	2 each	896
	4 to 17	G	2⅛"	2 each	56
	4 to 17	Tulip	template	-	168
	1st Border	-	2"	9	-
	2nd Border	-	3"	9	-
	3rd Border	-	4½"	9	-
Double	1	A	6½"	12	70
	2	B	2⅝"	5	140
	2	D	1¾"	18	140
	2	E	1¾"	12	140
	2	Leaf 1	template	-	140
	2	Leaf 2	template	-	70
	2	Leaf 3	template	-	70
	3	C	1¾"	3	70
	4 to 17	F	2⅜"	3 each	1120
	4 to 17	G	2⅛"	1 each	70
	4 to 17	Tulip	template	-	210
	1st Border	-	1½"	10	-
	2nd Border	-	3½"	10	-
	3rd Border	-	5½"	10	-

Quilt	Fabric #	Pattern Piece	Size of Strip	Number of Strips	Total Pieces Needed
Cutting the Strips Chart (continued)					
Queen	1	A	6½"	16	96
	2	B	2⅝"	6	192
	2	D	1¾"	24	192
	2	E	1¾"	16	192
	2	Leaf 1	template	-	192
	2	Leaf 2	template	-	96
	2	Leaf 3	template	-	96
	3	C	1¾"	4	96
	4 to 17	F	2⅜"	4 each	1536
	4 to 17	G	2⅛"	1 each	96
	4 to 17	Tulip	template	-	288
	1st Border	-	2½"	11	-
	2nd Border	-	4½"	11	-
	3rd Border	-	6½"	11	-
King	1	A	6½"	19	112
	2	B	2⅝"	7	224
	2	D	1¾"	28	224
	2	E	1¾"	19	224
	2	Leaf 1	template	-	224
	2	Leaf 2	template	-	112
	2	Leaf 3	template	-	112
	3	C	1¾"	5	112
	4 to 17	F	2⅜"	4 each	1792
	4 to 17	G	2⅛"	1 each	224
	4 to 17	Tulip	template	-	168
	1st Border	-	2½"	12	-
	2nd Border	-	6½"	12	-

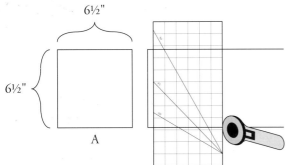

Cutting and Sewing the Pieces

Cut the strips indicated on the "Cutting the Strips" chart.

A Pieces. Divide the 6½" strips of fabric #1 into squares. See page 12 for cutting strips larger than 6".

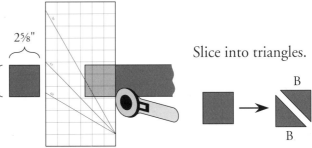

Slice into triangles.

B Pieces*. Divide the 2⅝" strips of fabric #2 into squares.

*or, use Easy Angle™. Cut the strips 2¼".

C Pieces. Divide the 1¾" strips fabric #3 into squares.

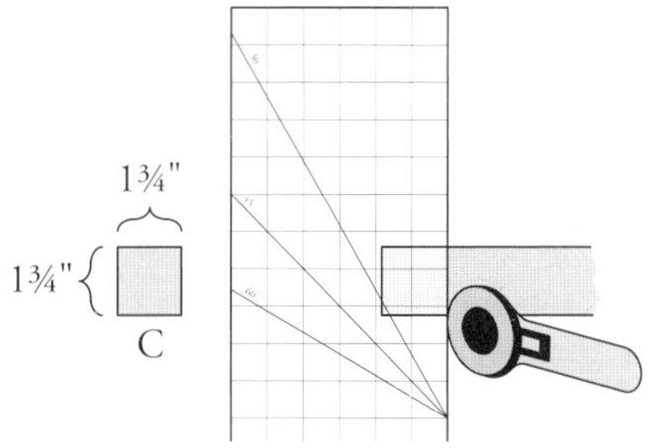

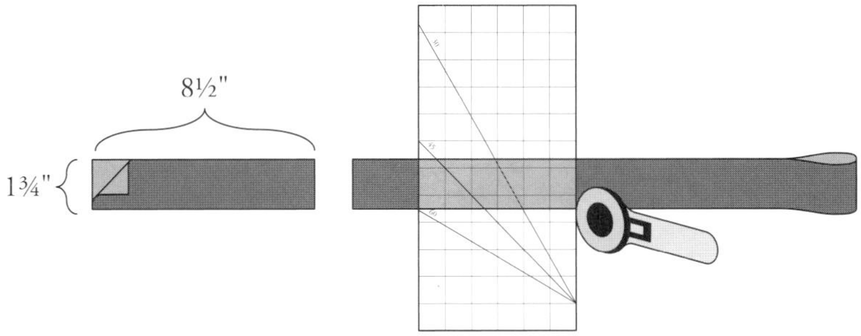

D Pieces. Divide the folded 1¾" strips of fabric #2 into rectangles every 8½".

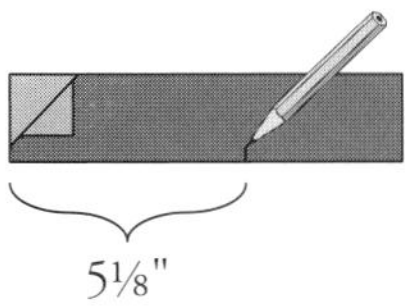

Keeping the 2 layers together, measure 5⅛" on the rectangles and mark with a dot. Lay your ruler with the 45° line along the bottom strip, with the cutting edge at the dot. Slice. You will have both the piece and its reverse.

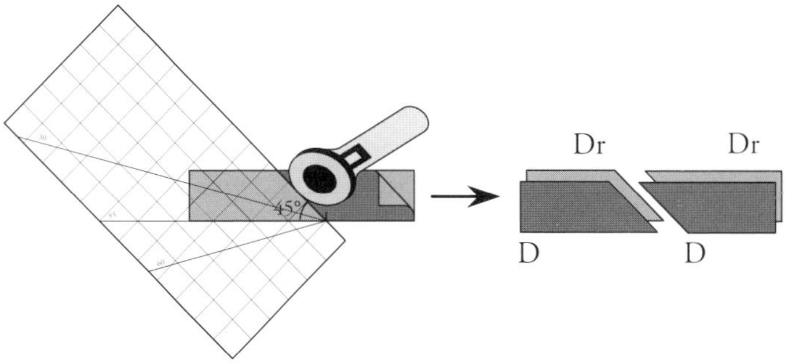

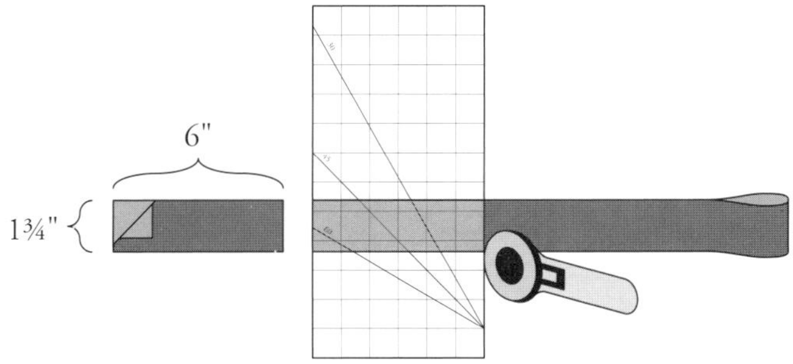

E Pieces. Divide the folded 1¾" strips of fabric #2 into rectangles every 6".

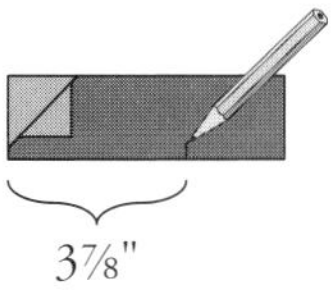

Keeping the 2 layers together, measure 3⅞" along the bottom edge of the rectangles and mark with a dot. Slice at a 45° angle. You will have **E** and **Er** pieces.

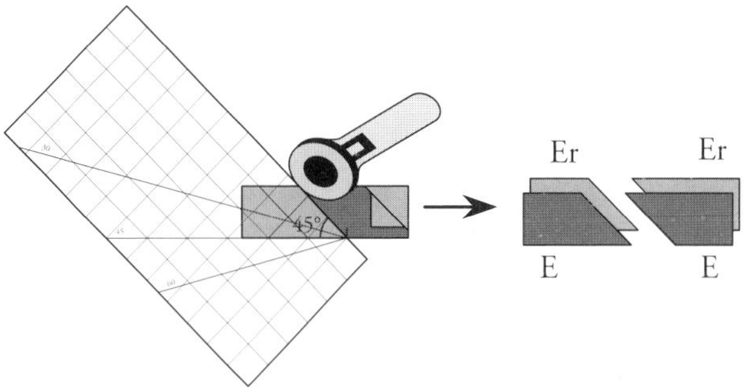

F Pieces. **F** pieces are made up of both individual pieces and sandwich-pieced triangles. Use the chart below to see how many pieces are needed for the two types of **F** pieces, and how many strips are required for each.

Piece F Chart					
	Wall	Twin	Double	Queen	King
Individual triangles from each fabric (#4-17)	14	32	40	56	64
Number of strips of each fabric (#4-17)	½ strip	1 strip	1½ strips	2 strips	2 strips
Sandwich-pieced pairs of triangles from each fabric set	96	224	280	384	448
Number of strips of each fabric (#4-17)	½ strip	1 strip	1½ strips	2 strips	2 strips

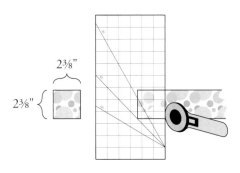

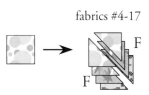

F Pieces, continued. Divide individual **F** strips into 2⅜" squares. Slice diagonally into triangles. Don't cut more than specified in the chart!

fabrics #4-17

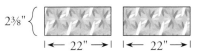

Sandwich-pieced **F** Pieces. The remaining **F** pieces will be sandwich–pieced triangles. See "Rules to Cut By" page 10. To get a real "scrappy" look, cut your remaining 2⅜" strips in half crosswise. This will give you more color combinations. Randomly pick up 2 half-strips at a time and sew them right sides together on both edges lengthwise.

Divide into squares.

Slice diagonally into triangles. Open and press seam to one side.

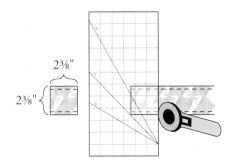

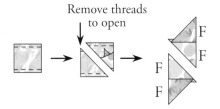

G Pieces. All these triangles are sandwich-pieced. You'll need 2 pairs for each block. Cut the long 2⅛" strips in half crosswise as you did for piece **F** to get more color combinations. Randomly pick up 2 half-strips at a time and sew the right sides together on both edges lengthwise.

Divide into squares.

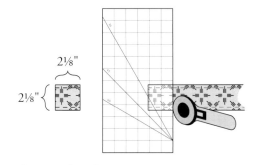

Slice diagonally into triangles.

Open and press seams to one side.

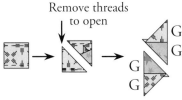

Assembling the Block

Sew **B** triangles onto 2 corners of your **A** square as shown. Let's call this Unit **AB**. Set aside.

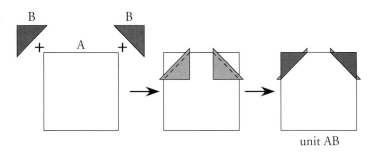

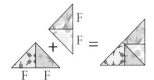

To piece the larger unit of **F** triangles, sew your pairs of **F** sandwich-pieced triangles together in twos.

Now sew two of these together to give you 8 triangles in each unit. Let's call this Large Unit **F**. Set aside.

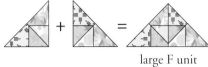

large F unit

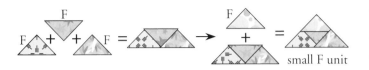

small F unit

To make the smaller unit of **F** triangles, sew the individual **F** triangles together as shown. Let's call this Small Unit **F**.

Sew together as shown to the right.

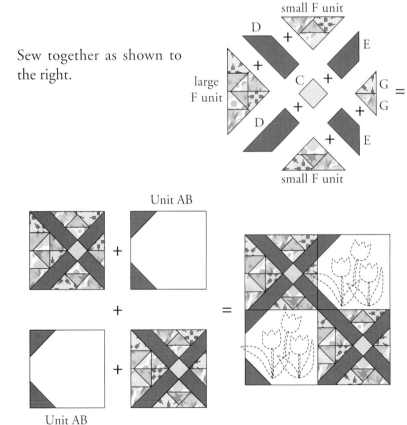

Sew the 4 sections together to finish the block.

Appliqué

Tulips. These will be hand appliquéd onto the individual blocks before they are sewn together with the exception of leaf #1. As you can see, some of these leaves overlap into the next block or the borders. Appliqué these up to ½" from the edge of the block and end with a knot on the back. Later, after the quilt top is sewn together, go back and finish appliquéing them.

If you need placement lines, lightly draw tulips onto all **AB** units. To do this, tape the pattern to a sunny window or a lightbox. Place the blocks over the pattern, right side up and trace the tulips onto the fabric with a very light pencil line. Usually it's best to trace just inside the design lines so the pencil won't show. Trace leaves and tulip pieces onto a plastic template sheet and cut them out.

Note: Make sure **AB** units are turned the correct way before tracing.

Trace around the appliqué templates on the right side of fabrics. This line will be your "turning under" or "sewing" line.

To add seam allowances, cut ¼" outside drawn line. You don't need to measure, just "eye" it.

Use the picture as a guide for clipping the tulips. This will enable you to turn seam allowances under without any puckering. Clip almost to the lines, not through them. The leaves don't need clipping at all, unless you want to make a few clips on the inside curves.

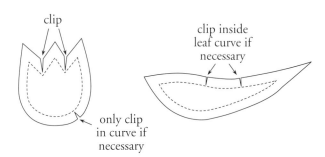

Stems. To make these, cut bias strips 1" wide. You will need about 22" of stem for each block, so multiply that by how many blocks you have and that will tell you how many total inches of bias strips you'll need. This doesn't need to be in one long strip – several small ones will be fine.

Fold the strips lengthwise, wrong sides together and sew with a ¼" seam. Trim the seam to ⅛" and center it along the middle back of the strip. Press the seam to one side. (A ¼" pressing bar is nice for this step if you have one.) Cut your strips apart as needed for the stems.

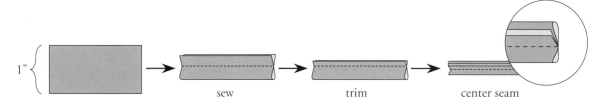

For hand appliqué, we prefer a Piecemakers® Hand Appliqué needle, or a #10 or #12 quilting needle. This will give you very thin, smooth stitches. The thinner the needle, the easier your sewing will be. Fat needles make you struggle too much, so avoid them! You may need to use a needle threader for these small needles, but it's worth it for the quality of work you'll get. Use the following steps:

> 1) Study the pattern and see which pieces need to go down first. You always work from the background to the foreground. The appliqué order for this block is: stems; middle left leaf; middle right leaf; far right leaf; far left leaf (except for tip); tulips.
>
> 2) Take the first piece to be appliquéd and lay it in its proper place. Stick a pin through some point on your drawn line and line it up with the corresponding place on the background. Do this in at least one more place to line it up.

Thread needle with about 18" of thread to match your first fabric.

Sew the piece in place using a blindstitch. To blindstitch, knot single thread. Fold seam allowance under so that your drawn line is just slightly underneath. Coming up from the back, bring needle through edge of fold.

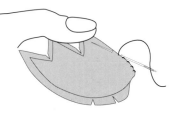

The needle goes back down in background fabric directly beside where you came up. Take about ⅛" stitch underneath and come back up catching the edge of fold again; continue.

Edges not seen need not be sewn under. They can lie flat underneath each overlapping piece. Keep adding each piece in order, changing thread colors to match each fabric.

Follow the "Sewing the Quilt Top Together" section on pages 14-15 to complete your quilt top.

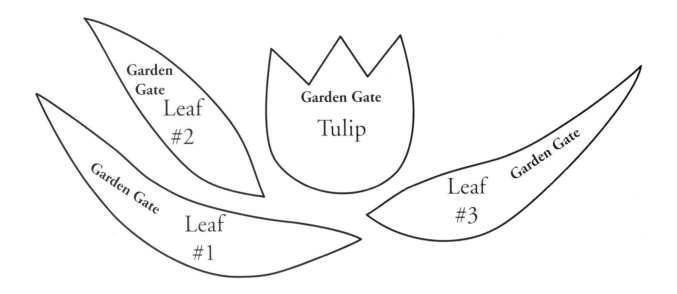

Garden Gate
Leaf #2

Garden Gate
Tulip

Garden Gate
Leaf #1

Leaf #3
Garden Gate

Presidential Platform 1992

An unusual block because it has no center and flows in several different directions, Presidential Platform 1992 is well-suited for less traditional projects as well as quilts. We chose to use this design as the focal point of a jacket pictured on page 62. Then we broke apart the design and filled in the rest of the jacket area with portions of the block and strips of fabric. Also, on page 97 is a drawing of a four block wallhanging, which shows a more complete design for a quilt.

We will begin by giving you instructions for construction of the block followed by general directions for designing the jacket. This block is for an experienced sewer!

See photograph page 62.

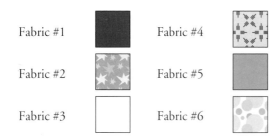

Fabric #1   Fabric #4

Fabric #2   Fabric #5

Fabric #3   Fabric #6

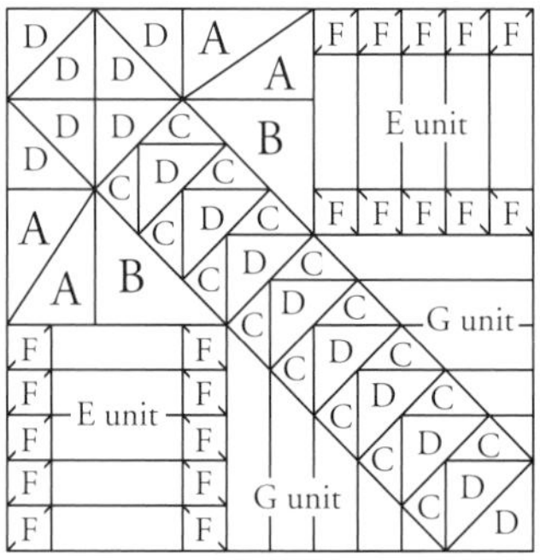

Yardage Chart					
	Small Wall	**Twin**	**Double**	**Queen**	**King**
	2 x 2	**4 x 7**	**5 x 7**	**6 x 8**	**7 x 8**
Fabric #					
1	1	2¾	3⅔	4⅞	5⅛
2	⅓	1	1¼	1⅝	1⅞
2 to 6 each	⅓	⅞	1	1⅜	1⅝
Borders (finished sizes given)					
1st Border	1" – ¼	1½" – ⅝	1" – ½	2" – ⅞	2" – ⅞
2nd Border	3" – ½	2½" – ⅞	3" – 1	4" – 1½	6" – 2⅛
3rd Border	-	4" – 1⅛	5" – 1⅝	6" – 2	-
Batting	1	6	6	6¼	9
Back	1	6	6⅛	8	9
Binding	¾	1	1	1	1¼
Finished Size	32" x 32"	64" x 100"	78" x 102"	84" x 108"	100" x 112"

Cutting the Strips					
Quilt	Fabric #	Pattern Piece	Size of Strip	Number of Strips	Total Pieces Needed
Small Wall	1	A	2¾"	1	8
	1	C	3¼"	2	64
	1	D	2⅞"	1	16
	2	A	2¾"	1	8
	2	B	3⅞"	1	8
	2	D	2⅞"	1	16
	2 to 6	D	2⅞"	1 each	32
	2 to 6	Rectangle E	1½"	1 each	8
	2 to 6	Triangle G	1½"	1 each	8
	1st Border	-	1½"	-	4
	2nd Border	-	3½"	-	4
Twin	1	A	2¾"	3	56
	1	C	3¼"	10	448
	1	D	2⅞"	4	112
	2	A	2¾"	3	56
	2	B	3⅞"	3	56
	2	D	2⅞"	4	112
	2 to 6	D	2⅞"	2 each	224
	2 to 6	Rectangle E	1½"	5 each	56
	2 to 6	Triangle G	1½"	1 each	56
	1st Border	-	2"	-	9
	2nd Border	-	3"	-	9
	3rd Border	-	4½"	-	9
Double	1	A	2¾"	4	70
	1	C	3¼"	12	560
	1	D	2⅞"	5	140
	2	A	2¾"	4	70
	2	B	3⅞"	4	70
	2	D	2⅞"	5	140
	2 to 6	D	2⅞"	2 each	280
	2 to 6	Rectangle E	1½"	6 each	70
	2 to 6	Triangle G	1½"	5 each	70
	1st Border	-	1½"	-	10
	2nd Border	-	3½"	-	10
	3rd Border	-	5½"	-	10
Queen	1	A	2¾"	5	96
	1	C	3¼"	16	768
	1	D	2⅞"	7	192
	2	A	2¾"	5	96
	2	B	3⅞"	5	96
	2	D	2⅞"	7	192
	2 to 6	D	2⅞"	3 each	384
	2 to 6	Rectangle E	1½"	8 each	96
	2 to 6	Triangle G	1½"	7 each	96
	1st Border	-	2½"	-	11
	2nd Border	-	4½"	-	11
	3rd Border	-	6½"	-	11

			Cutting the Strips (continued)		
Quilt	Fabric #	Pattern Piece	Size of Strip	Number of Strips	Total Pieces Needed
King	1	A	2¾"	6	112
	1	C	3¼"	19	896
	1	D	2⅞"	8	224
	2	A	2¾"	6	112
	2	B	3⅞"	6	112
	2	D	2⅞"	8	224
	2 to 6	D	2⅞"	4 each	448
	2 to 6	Rectangle E	1½"	10 each	112
	2 to 6	Triangle G	1½"	8 each	112
	1st Border	-	2½""	-	12
	2nd Border	-	6½"	-	12

Note: Fabric #2 is listed individually and with fabrics #2 through #6. This is because it is treated individually in some portions of the block and as part of a set of strips or Flying Geese in another. In the jacket pictured on page 62, we used red as fabric #2.

Cutting and Sewing the Pieces

Cut the strips indicated on the "Cutting the Strips" chart.

Unit A.

Divide the folded 2¾" strips of fabrics #1 and #2 into rectangles every 4⅛". Make sure you divide and slice folded strips so you have **A** and **Ar** (reverse) pieces. This is called Unit **A**.

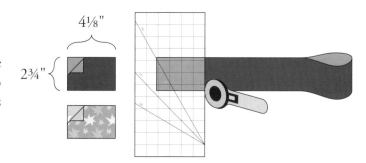

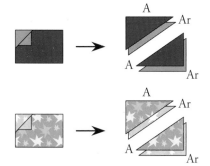

Slice diagonally into triangles.

Sew pairs of triangles together, fabric #1 to fabric #2.

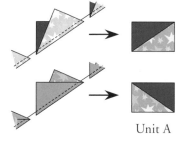

Unit A

B Pieces*. Divide the 3⅞" strips of fabric #2 into squares.　　Slice diagonally into triangles.

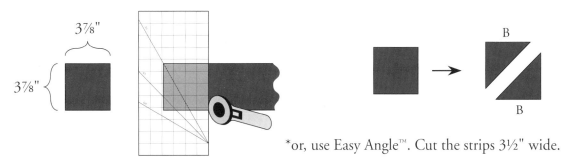

*or, use Easy Angle™. Cut the strips 3½" wide.

C Pieces*. Divide the 3¼" strips of fabric #1 into squares.　　Criss-cross slice into triangles.

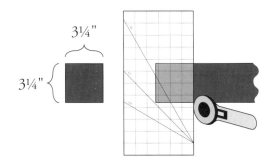

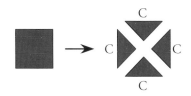

*or, use Companion Angle™. Cut the strips 1½" wide.

D Pieces*. Divide the 2⅞" strips of fabric #1 into squares. Slice diagonally into triangles. Divide the 2⅞" strips of fabric #2 through #6 into squares. Slice diagonally into triangles.

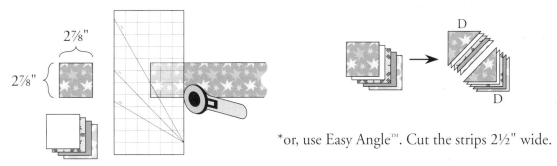

*or, use Easy Angle™. Cut the strips 2½" wide.

E Pieces. Sew 1½" strips of fabric #2 through #6 together in any order you wish. Press seams all one way. Divide your new 5½" "strips set" into rectangles every 3½".

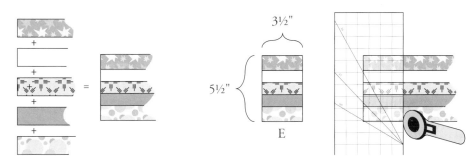

F Pieces*. These are all quick–pieced triangles. See page 11 of "Rules to Cut By" for drawing, sewing and cutting instructions.

*or, use 1" finished
SPEED GRIDS®

Use the chart below for square size and how many to draw of each fabric pair. Make separate grids by placing fabric #1 right sides together with each of fabrics #2 through #6.

Quilt Size	Wall	Twin	Double	Queen	King
Grid Size	1⅞"	1⅞"	1⅞"	1⅞"	1⅞"
# of squares across x down (for each pair of fabrics)	4 x 2	14 x 4	14 x 5	12 x 8	14 x 8

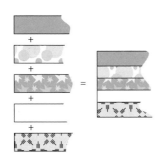

G Pieces. Sew 1½" strips of fabrics #2 through #6 together in any order you wish. Press seams all one way.

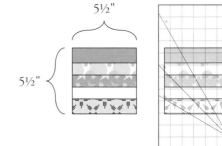

Divide your new 5½" "strip set" into 5½" squares.

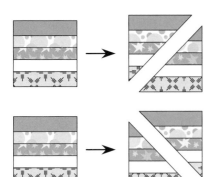

Slice squares into triangles.

Assembling the Block

Sew your block together following the steps below:

Using the **C** pieces of fabric #1 **and D** pieces of fabrics #2 through #6, construct eight units as shown. Sew these eight units into a strip in random order.

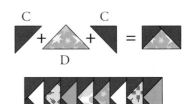

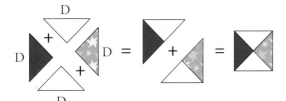

At the top, make a square from four **D** pieces.

Add one more **D** piece of fabric #2 on the left end. Add a **D** piece of fabric #1 at the right end.

96

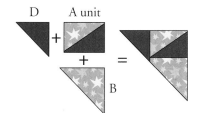

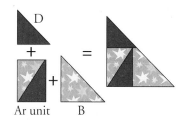

Piece **D** (fabric #1) to Unit **A** to **B**. Make one of each as shown here.

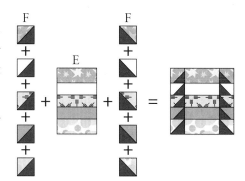

Using the order that strips are sewn in rectangle **E**, sew quick-pieced triangles together in the same order. Make four sets for a block, watching the direction the triangles sit as shown at the right.

Sew the sets of quick-pieced triangles to each side of the **E** rectangles.

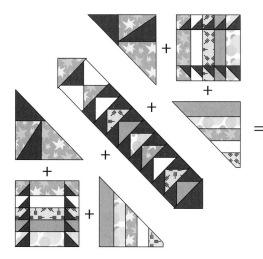

Sew the units together as shown.

Here is a drawing of four blocks of Presidential Platform 1992. This block can be turned several ways to create interesting designs.

Follow the "Sewing the Quilt Top Together" section on pages 14-15 to complete your quilt top.

Constructing the Jacket

Choose a jacket pattern. There are many wonderful patterns available which you can adapt to this method of construction.

The jacket will have three layers – the pieced top (where all your hard work is!), the batting(we used a flat batt) and the lining.

Cut out the jacket fronts, back, sleeves and collar from your batting and lining. The batting will be the foundation on which you will do all your piecing.

Construct basic ingredients for your pieced top. We constructed ours in the following steps:

1. Piece six Presidential Platform 1992 blocks.

2. Piece about 3 yards of the "flying geese" strip to break apart and use in various places.

3. Strip together 1½" strips of fabrics #2 through #6 and cut them into **G** triangles and piece several **D/A/B** triangle units.

4. Place the six blocks on the batting pieces.

5. Now fill in the space left. We began our designing with the back. It is the largest area and usually the easiest to visualize. You can use the "flying geese" strip, **G** triangles, **D/A/B** triangles and leftover 1½" strips of fabric to fill in.

Jacket Back

Jacket Front

Jacket Sleeves – Make 2

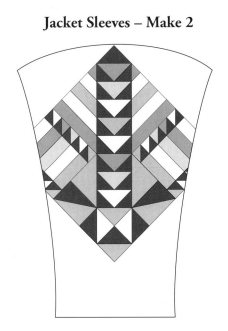

The front and back of our jacket was so full of activity that we chose to fill in the blank sleeve area with 1½" black strips only.

We used a "flying geese" strip for the collar.

If you are unsure of how something will look, machine baste it down first. That way it can easily be pulled off if you don't like it.

After piecing your jacket top onto the batting, machine quilt if you desire, and then follow the jacket pattern for completing the jacket.

What fun to create a masterpiece that you can wear!

Spun Gold

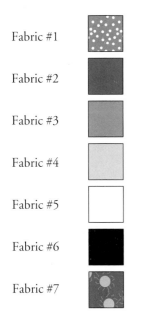

Fabric #1

Fabric #2

Fabric #3

Fabric #4

Fabric #5

Fabric #6

Fabric #7

Spinning stars are the theme for this quilt! They seem to twinkle in and out of the bigger stars making this quilt a delight for any age. This pattern is for someone who has had piecing experience.

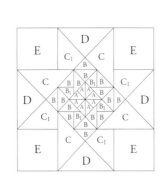

See photograph on page 57.

The yardage chart below is for blocks that are set straight. The quilt pictured on page 57 was set on point. If you want to make the wall quilt shown on page 57, make eight blocks and get one extra yard of fabric #6 for the large background triangles.

		Wall 3 x 3	Twin 4 x 7	Double 5 x 7	Queen 6 x 8	King 7 x 8
Yardage Chart						
Fabric						
	1	½	⅞	1⅛	1¼	1½
	2	¼	⅜	⅜	½	½
	3	¼	⅝	⅝	⅞	⅞
	4	⅛	⅓	⅓	½	⅝
	5	1	2⅞	3	4¼	4⅞
	6	⅜	1	1⅛	1½	1¾
	7	⅜	1	1⅛	1½	¾
Borders (finished sizes given)						
1st Border		1" – ⅓	1½" – ½	1" – ½	2" – ⅞	2" – ⅞
2nd Border		4" – ⅞	2½" – ¾	3" – 1	4" – 1½	6" – 2
3rd Border		4" – 1⅛	5" – 1⅝	6" – 2	-	-
Batting		1½	6	6	6¼	9
Back 3		6	6⅛	8	9	-
Binding		¾	1	1	1	1¼
Finished Size		46"x 46"	64" x 100"	78" x 102"	84" x 108"	100" x 112"

Cutting the Strips					
Quilt	Fabric #	Pattern Piece	Size of Strip	Number of Strips	Total Pieces Needed
Wall	1	B	2⅜"	2	36
	3	B	3"	2	36
	4	B	2⅜"	1	36
	5	D	6¼"	2	36
	5	E	4"	4	36
	6	C	4⅜"	2	36
	7	C1	4⅜"	2	36
Twin	1	B	2⅜"	4	112
	3	B	3"	5	112
	4	B	2⅜"	3	112
	5	D	6¼"	5	112
	5	E	4"	12	112
	6	C	4⅜"	7	112
	7	C1	4⅜"	7	112
Double	1	B	2⅜"	5	140
	3	B	3"	6	140
	4	B	2⅜"	3	140
	5	D	6¼"	6	140
	5	E	4"	14	140
	6	C	4⅜"	8	140
	7	C1	4⅜"	8	140
Queen	1	B	2⅜"	6	192
	3	B	3"	8	192
	4	B	2⅜"	4	192
	5	D	6¼"	8	192
	5	E	4"	20	192
	6	C	4⅜"	11	192
	7	C1	4⅜"	11	192
King	1	B	2⅜"	7	224
	3	B	3"	9	224
	4	B	2⅜"	5	224
	5	D	6¼"	10	224
	5	E	4"	23	224
	6	C	4⅜"	13	224
	7	C1	4⅜"	13	224

Cutting and Sewing the Pieces

Cut the strips indicated on the Strip Cutting Chart.

A Pieces*. These are quick-pieced triangles. See "Rules to Cut By" chapter for drawing, sewing and cutting instructions. Use chart to the right for drawing grids. Draw squares 1⅞" using fabrics #1 and #2.

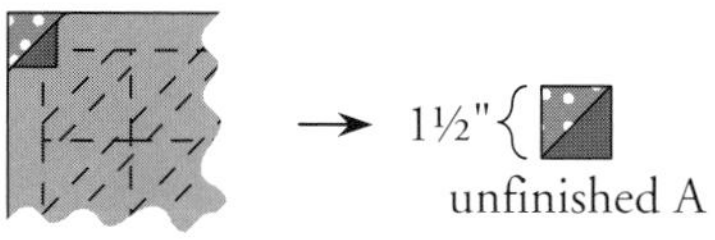

* or use 1" finished
SPEED GRIDS®
1½"
unfinished A

Quilt Size	Wall	Twin	Double	Queen	King
Grid Size	1⅞"	1⅞"	1⅞"	1⅞"	1⅞"
# of Squares across x down	9 x 4	14 x 8	20 x 7	16 x 12	16 x 14

B Pieces. Some of these are quick-pieced triangles, some are cut individually, and some are sandwich-pieced triangles. Follow the steps below for cutting.

Quick-pieced **B** triangles. See "Rules to Cut By" chapter for drawing, sewing and cutting instructions. Use chart below for drawing grids. Draw squares 2⅜" using fabrics #1 and #5.

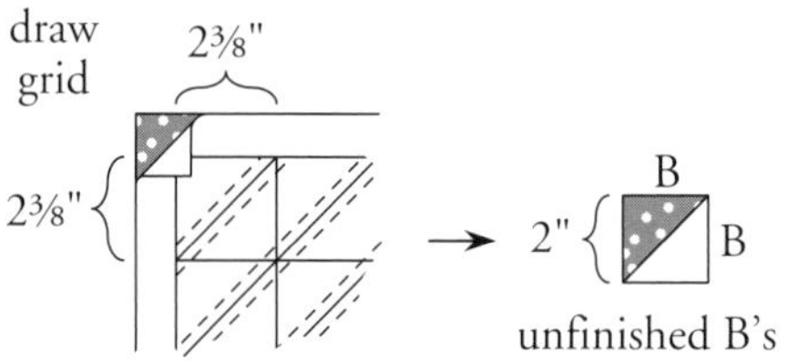

draw
grid
2⅜"
2⅜"
2"
B
B
unfinished B's

Quilt Size	Wall	Twin	Double	Queen	King
Grid Size	2⅜"	2⅜"	2⅜"	2⅜"	2⅜"
# of Squares across x down	9 x 4	14 x 8	20 x 7	16 x 12	16 x 14

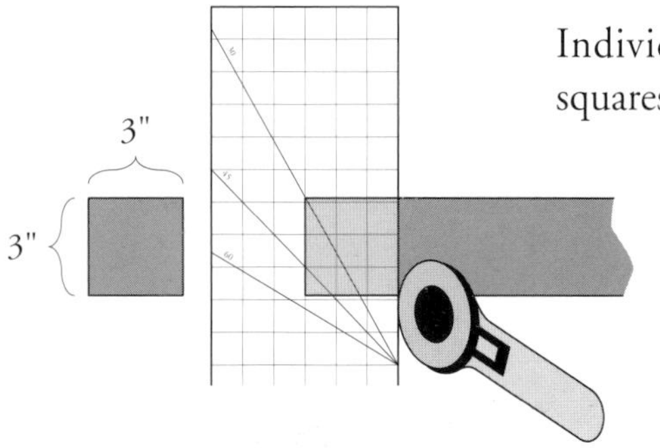

3"
3"

Individual **B** pieces. Divide the strips 3" strips of fabric #3 into squares. Slice into triangles.

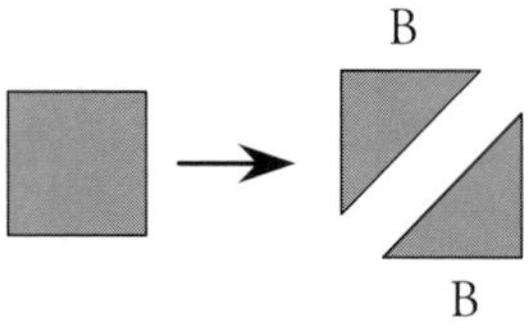

B
B

Sandwich-pieced **B** triangles. Lay 2⅜" strips of fabricis #1 and #4 right sides together. Sew lengthwise along both sides. Refer to page 10 for complete instructions. Divide into squares, then slice diagonally into triangles.

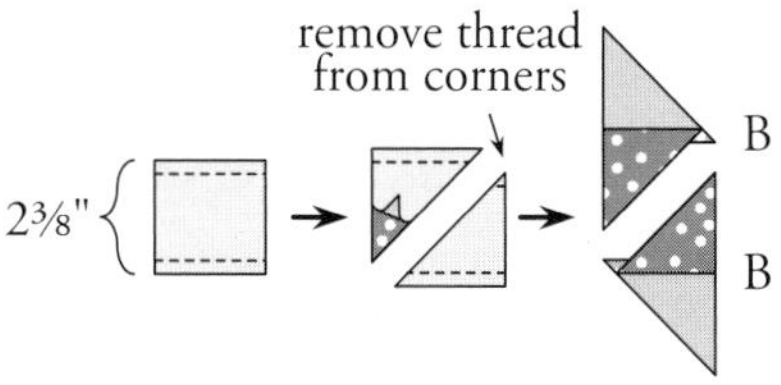

remove thread
from corners
2⅜"
B
B

C Pieces. Individual **C** pieces. Divide the 4⅜" strips of fabrics #6 and #7 into squares. Slice diagonally into triangles.

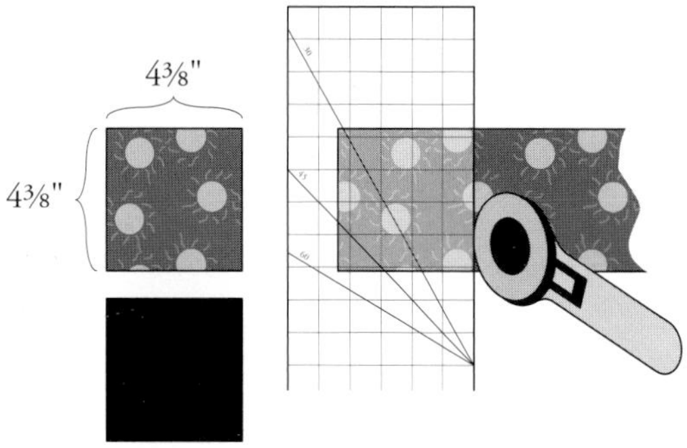

4⅜"
4⅜"

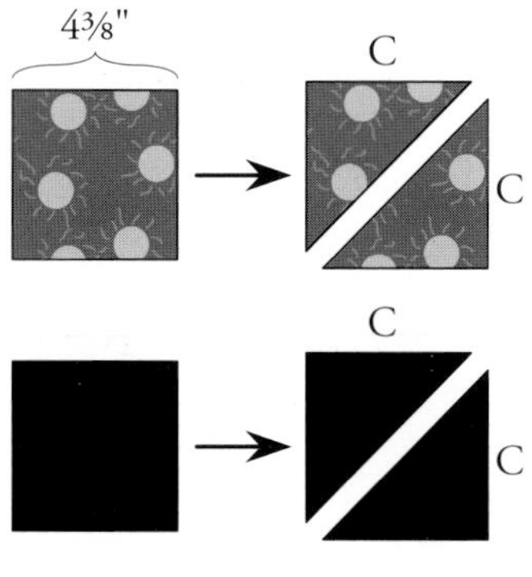

4⅜"
C
C
C
C

C1 Pieces. These are a slight variation of the **C** pieces. Using the triangles cut from fabric #6 in the previous step, measure 1¾" along base and cut off perpendicular to base.

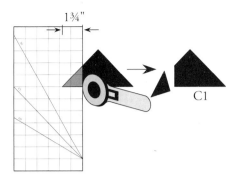

D Pieces. Divide the 6¼" strips of fabric #5 into squares. To cut wider strips than your ruler, see "General Guidelines" page 12. Criss-cross slice into triangles.

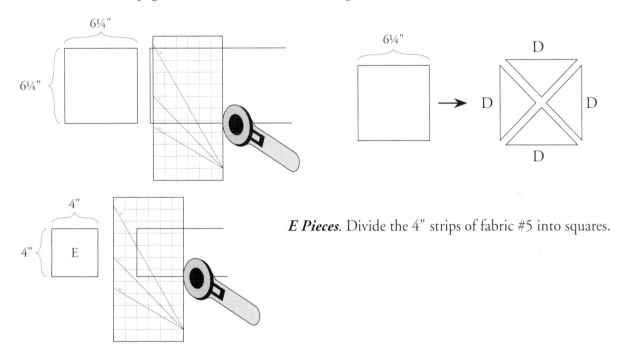

E Pieces. Divide the 4" strips of fabric #5 into squares.

Assembling the Block

Sew the block together following the steps below.

> Sew center **A** pieces in pairs. Sew the pairs together to form a center pinwheel. Set aside.

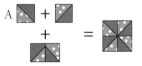

To make the small star units that go around the center pinwheel, sew an individual **B** triangle of fabric #3 to the sandwich-pieced **B** unit of fabrics #1 and #4. Take a "fat" ¼" seam allowance on this step only!

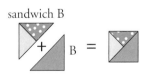

Take a "fat" ¼" seam allowance on this step only!

Slice ⅝" off the bottom of the whole unit, slicing across fabrics #3 and #4. Make four units.

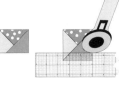

Sew the corner quick-pieced triangles **B** triangles on two of the **B/sandwich B** units to make the top and bottom rows for the center square.

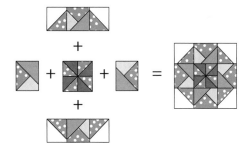

Sew the other two **B/sandwich B** units to the center pinwheel to make the middle row for the center square.

Sew the top and bottom rows to the middle to make the center square.

Sew **E/C/C1** units together. Make four.

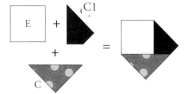

Sew **D** triangles on two of the **E/C/C1** units to make top and bottom triangles. Set aside.

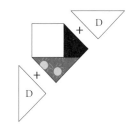

Sew the other two **E/C/C1** units onto the sides of the center square.

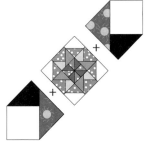

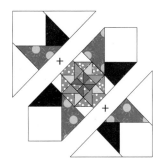

Sew the **E/C/C1/D** triangles to the top and bottom of the center square.

Follow the "Sewing the Quilt Top Together" section on pages 14-15 to complete your quilt top.

As an option, you can sew the blocks together diagonally "on-point" as pictured on page 57.

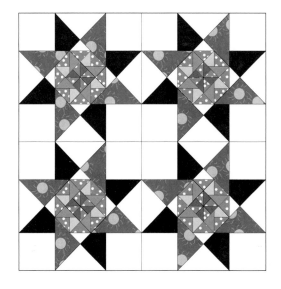

Spun Gold

Diagonal Setting for Wallhanging

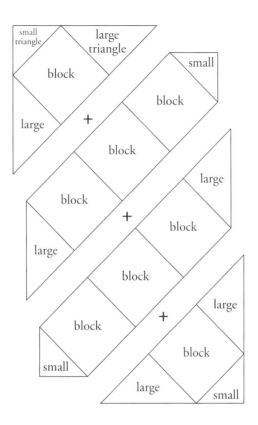

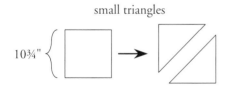

small triangles

10¾" {

Small Triangles. Draw two squares 10¾". Slice diagonally and you will have four triangles.

Large Triangles. Draw two squares 21". Criss-cross slice and you will have a total of eight triangles. You only need six of them.

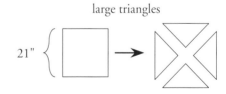

large triangles

21" {

Windy

This is an intermediate quilt for someone who has machine piecing experience. You'll do some "angle" cutting with your ruler, which is not difficult once you get the hang of it. Windy is a great pattern to experiment with color shading as it forms a secondary pattern when the blocks are put together.

See photograph page 58.

Fabric #1

Fabric #2

Fabric #3

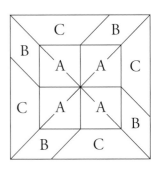

Yardage Chart					
	Wall	**Twin**	**Double**	**Queen**	**King**
	3 x 3	**4 x 7**	**5 x 7**	**6 x 8**	**7 x 8**
Fabric #					
1	1⅓	3¼	3¾	4⅜	5
2	⅝	1¼	1⅜	2	2¼
3	⅝	1¼	1⅜	2	2¼
Border (finished sizes given)					
1st Border	1" – ⅓	1½" – ⅝	1" – ½	2" – ⅞	2" – ⅞
2nd Border	4" – ⅞	2½" – ⅞	3" – 1⅛	4" – 1½	6" – 2⅛
3rd Border	-	4" – 1¼	5" – 1⅔	6" – 2⅛	-
Batting	1½	6	6	6¼	9
Backing	3	6	6⅛	8	9
Binding	¾	1	1	1	1¼
Finished Size	46" x 46"	64" x 100"	78" x 102"	84" x 108"	100" x 112"

		Cutting the Strips Chart			
Quilt	Fabric #	Pattern Piece	Size of Strip	Number of Strips	Total Pieces Needed
Wall	1	C	3"	6	36
	2	B	3"	3	18
	3	B	3"	3	18
	1st Border	-	1½"	6	-
	2nd Border	-	4½"	6	-
Twin	1	C	3"	19	112
	2	B	3"	7	56
	3	B	3"	7	56
	1st Border	-	2"	9	-
	2nd Border	-	3"	9	-
	3rd Border	-	4½"	9	-
Double	1	C	3"	24	140
	2	B	3"	9	70
	3	B	3"	9	70
	1st Border	-	1½"	10	-
	2nd Border	-	3½"	10	-
	3rd Border	-	5½"	10	-
Queen	1	C	3"	32	192
	2	B	3"	12	96
	3	B	3"	12	96
	1st Border	-	2½"	11	-
	2nd Border	-	4½"	11	-
	3rd Border	-	6½"	11	-
King	1	C	3"	38	224
	2	B	3"	14	112
	3	B	3"	14	112
	1st Border	-	2½"	12	-
	2nd Border	-	6½"	12	-

Cutting and Sewing the Pieces

Cut strips indicated on "Cutting the Strips" chart.

Unit A.

This center pinwheel is made with quick-pieced triangles. See page 11 of "Rules to Cut By" chapter for drawing, sewing and cutting instructions.

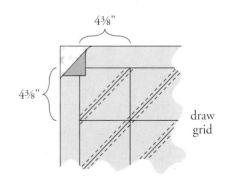

4⅜"

4⅜"

draw grid

You will be drawing two identical grids. Lay the following pairs of fabrics right sides together: #1 and #2 and #1 and #3.

4"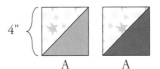

Refer to the chart for drawing both grids. Your squares will be 4⅜".

Quilt Size	Wall	Twin	Double	Queen	King
Grid Size	4⅜"	4⅜"	4⅜"	4⅜"	4⅜"
# of Squares across x down	3 x 3	7 x 4	9 x 4	9 x 6	9 x 7

B Diamond Pieces*. You will use the 3" strips of fabrics #2 and #3 for this step. Lay the 45° line on the ruler along the bottom edge of a folded strip. Slice the angle on the right side.

3"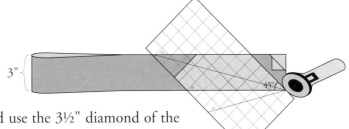

*or, use Easy Eight™. Cut strips 3" wide and use the 3½" diamond of the Easy Eight™ to cut pieces.

4¼"

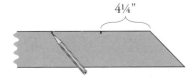

Measure every 4¼" along the top edge of the strip and mark with dots.

Now lay the 45° line on the bottom of the strip with the cutting edge of the ruler at the first dot. Slice diamond and continue slicing at each dot.

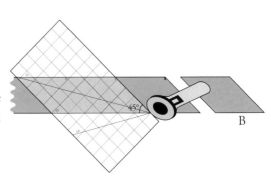

C Pieces. Cut the selvages off the 3" strip of fabric #1.

3"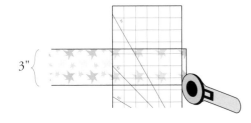

Mark strip with dots alternately at 9¾" and 3¾" intervals, beginning with 9¾" on the right bottom side.

9¾" 3¾" 9¾"

Lay the 45° line of the ruler along the bottom of the strip, with the cutting edge at the bottom right edge of the strip. Slice.

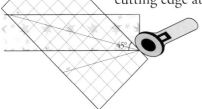

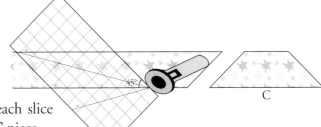

Alternate the direction of the ruler with each slice to achieve the "flat pyramid" shape of the **C** piece.

Assembling the Block

Sew the block together following the diagrams:

a. Sew four **A** units to make the pinwheel center.

b. Piece **B**'s to **C**'s.

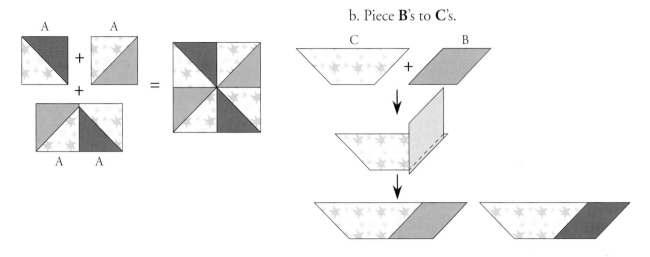

Attach **B/C** units to center pinwheel.

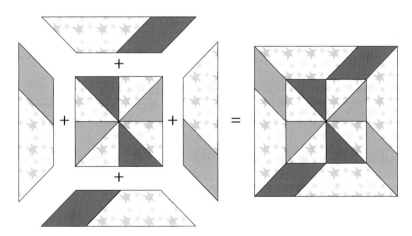

Follow the "Sewing the Quilt Top Together" section on pages 14-15 to complete your quilt top.

Blast Off!

Fabric #1

Fabric #2

Fabric #3

Fabric #4

Fabric #5

Fabric #6

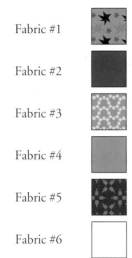

As sharp as a rocket blasting off, this pattern is great for using lots of bright colors. An intermediate to advanced piecer will have lots of fun with this one.

See photograph page 50.

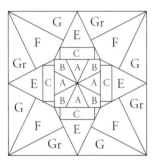

D and Dr pieces not labeled

Yardage Chart						
	Small Wall **2 x 2**	**Wall** **3 x 3**	**Twin** **4 x 7**	**Double** **5 x 7**	**Queen** **6 x 8**	**King** **7 x 8**
Fabric #						
1	¼	¼	⅜	½	⅔	¾
2	¼	¼	⅝	¾	1	1⅛
3	⅛	¼	½	⅝	¾	⅞
4	¼	½	1	1⅓	1⅔	1⅞
5	⅓	⅝	1⅝	1⅞	2⅜	2¾
6	½	⅔	2	2⅜	3⅛	3⅔
Border (finished sizes given)						
1st Border	1" – ¼	1" – ⅓	1½" – ⅝	1" – ½	2" – ⅞	2" – ⅞
2nd Border	3" – ½	4" – ⅞	2½" – ⅞	3" – 1	4" – 1½	6" – 2⅛
3rd Border	-	-	4" – 1⅛	5" – 1⅝	6" – 2	-
Batting	1	1½	6	6	6¼	9
Back	1	3	6	6⅛	8	9
Binding	¾	¾	1	1	1	1¼
Finished Size	32" x 32"	46" x 46"	64" x 100"	78" x 102"	84" x 108"	100" x 112"

		Cutting the Strips			
Quilt	Fabric #	Pattern Piece	Size of Strip	Number of Strips	Total Pieces Needed
Small Wallhanging	1	A	2¾"	1	16
	2	B	template	-	16
	3	C	1½"	2	16
	4	D	1⅛"	1	32
	4	E	3¾"	1	16
	5	F	template	-	16
	6	G	3⅜"	3	32
	1st Border	-	1½"	4	-
	2nd Border	-	3½"	4	-
Wallhanging	1	A	2¾"	2	36
	2	B	template	-	36
	3	C	1½"	3	36
	4	D	1⅛"	3	72
	4	E	3¾"	2	36
	5	F	template	-	36
	6	G	3⅜"	6	72
	1st Border	-	1½"	6	-
	2nd Border	-	4½"	6	-
Twin	1	A	2¾"	4	112
	2	B	template	-	112
	3	C	1½"	10	112
	4	D	1⅛"	7	224
	4	E	3¾"	6	112
	5	F	template	-	112
	6	G	3⅜"	19	224
	1st Border	-	2"	9	-
	2nd Border	-	3"	9	-
	3rd Border	-	4½"	9	-
Double	1	A	2¾"	5	140
	2	B	template	-	140
	3	C	1½"	12	140
	4	D	1⅛"	9	280
	4	E	3¾"	8	140
	5	F	template	-	140
	6	G	3⅜"	24	280
	1st Border	-	1½"	10	-
	2nd Border	-	3½"	10	-
	3rd Border	-	5½"	10	-

Cutting the Strips (continued)					
Quilt	Fabric #	Pattern Piece	Size of Strip	Number of Strips	Total Pieces Needed
Queen	1	A	2¾"	7	192
	2	B	template	-	192
	3	C	1½"	16	192
	4	D	1⅛"	12	384
	4	E	3¾"	11	192
	5	F	template	-	192
	6	G	3⅜"	32	384
	1st Border	-	2½"	11	-
	2nd Border	-	4½"	11	-
	3rd Border	-	6½"	11	-
King	1	A	2¾"	8	224
	2	B	template	-	224
	3	C	1½"	19	224
	4	D	1⅛"	14	448
	4	E	3¾"	12	224
	5	F	template	-	224
	6	G	3⅜"	38	448
	1st Border	-	2½"	12	-
	2nd Border	-	6½"	12	-

Cutting the Pieces

Cut the strips using the "Cutting the Strips" chart.

A Pieces. Trace your A template onto the 2¾" strips of fabric #1 as shown. The tip will hang slightly off the edge each time.

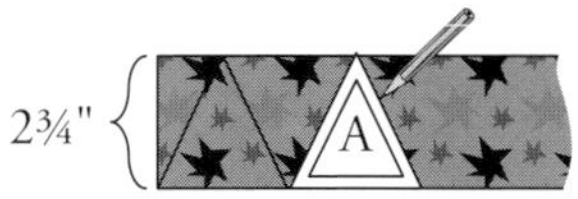
2¾"
A

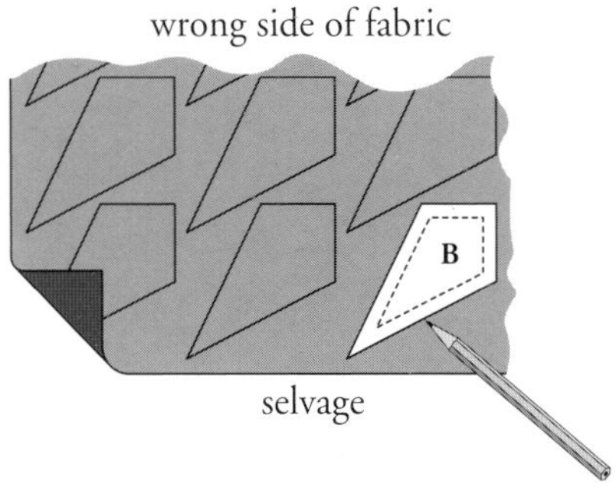
wrong side of fabric
B
selvage

B Pieces. There are no strips for these pieces. Use your **B** template and fabric #2. Draw around the template and cut on the line – seam allowances are already included. You can cut several layers at a time.

C Pieces. Divide the 1½" strips of fabric #3 into rectangles every 3½".

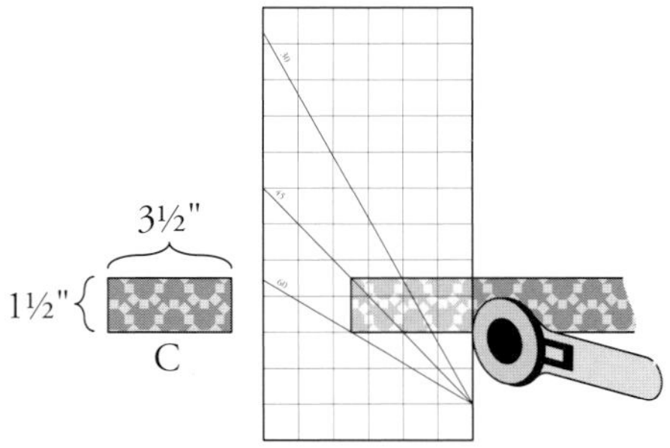
3½"
1½"
C

D Pieces. Divide the folded 1⅛" strip of fabric #4 into rectangles every 2⅜".

Slice diagonally into triangles. Make sure you keep the strips folded so you will have both **D** and **Dr** (D reverse) pieces.

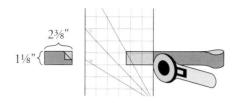

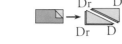

E Pieces. Trace your **E** template onto the 3¾" strips of fabric #4. The tips may hang slightly off the edge.

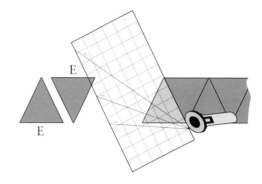

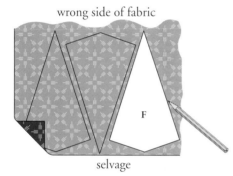

F Pieces. There are no strips of these pieces. Use your **F** template to draw the number of pieces needed of fabric #5 (see chart). You can cut several layers at a time because seam allowances are included on the template.

G Pieces. Divide the folded 3⅜" strips of fabric #6 into rectangles every 6¾". To cut strips wider than your ruler, see "General Guidelines" page 12.

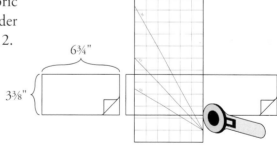

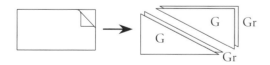

Slice diagonally into triangles. Using the folded strip will give you **G** and **Gr** (G reverse).

Assembling the Block

Piece center like this. Make two halves.

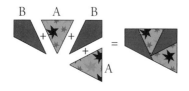

Sew the two halves together.

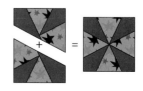

113

Sew four **D/C/Dr** units.

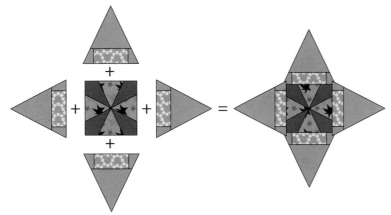

Sew the four **E** pieces to the tops of the **D/C/Dr** units.

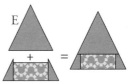

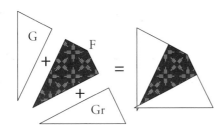

Attach the **E/D/C/Dr** unit to the center unit.

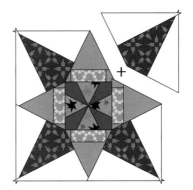

Sew the four **G/F/Gr** corner units.

Set the **G/F/Gr** units into the corners.

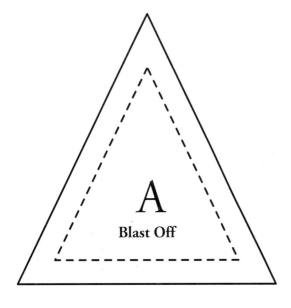

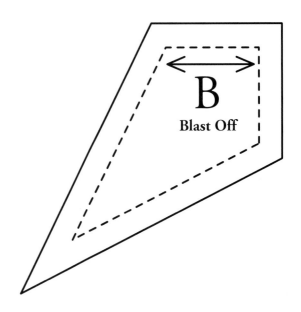

Follow the "Sewing the Quilt Top Together" section on pages 14-15 to complete your quilt top.

A
Blast Off

B
Blast Off

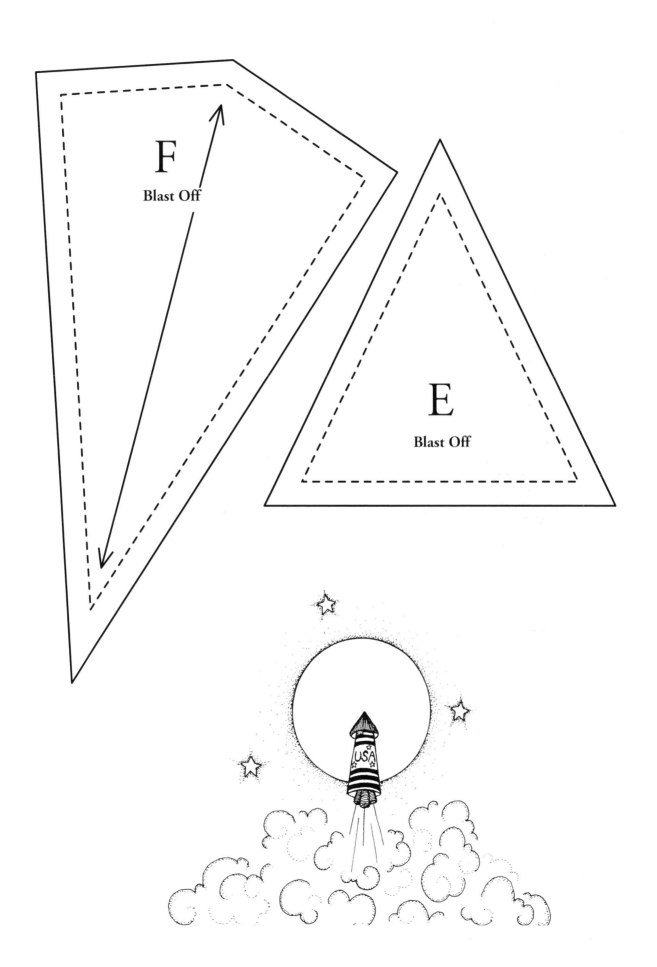

F

Blast Off

E

Blast Off

Star Chamber

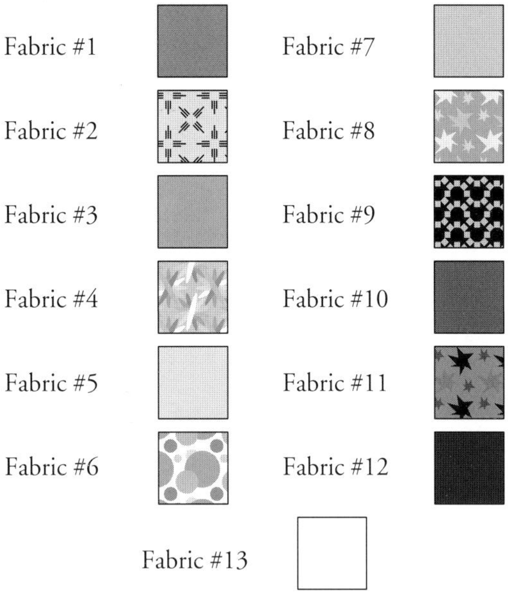

Fabric #1  Fabric #7

Fabric #2 Fabric #8

Fabric #3 Fabric #9

Fabric #4  Fabric #10

Fabric #5 Fabric #11

Fabric #6 Fabric #12

Fabric #13

This is a delightful pattern that lends itself perfectly to a memory or friendship quilt. The background areas make snowflake–like stars that give just enough space for a message. We used a permanent Pigma fabric pen to write on our quilt. You can also embroider your messages if you like.

You get a wonderful "scrappy" look by using eight different fabrics of the same intensity for the diamonds and four different fabrics for the triangles. This pattern leaves lots of room for creativity!

See photograph page 59.

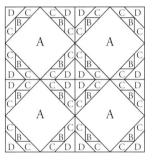

Yardage Chart					
	Wall 3 x 3	**Twin** 4 x 7	**Double** 5 x 7	**Queen** 6 x 8	**King** 7 x 8
Fabrics #					
1 to 8	⅛ yd. each	⅓ yd. each	⅓ yd. each	½ yd. each	½ yd. each
9 to 12	¼ yd. each	⅜ yd. each	½ yd. each	½ yd. each	⅝ yd. each
13	1	2¾	3⅜	4⅝	5¼
Borders (finished sizes given)					
1st Border	1" – ⅓	1½" – ½	1" – ½	2" – ⅞	2" – ¾
2nd Border	4" – ⅞	2½ " – ¾	3" – 1	4" – 1"	6" – 2
3rd Border	-	4" – 1⅛	5" – 1⅝	6"– 2	-
Batting	1½	6	6 yd	6¼	9
Back	3	6	6⅛	8	9
Binding	¾	1	1	1	1¼
Finished Size	46" x 46"	64" x 100"	78" x 102"	84" x 108"	100" x 112"

			Cutting the Strips		
Quilt	Fabric #	Pattern Piece	Size of Strip	Number of Strips	Total Pieces Needed
Wall	1 to 8	C	1⅜"	2 each	288
	9 to 12	D	2⅝"	2 each	114
	13	A	4¾"	5	36
	13	B	2⅛"	4	114
	1st Border	-	1½"	6	-
	2nd Border	-	4½"	6	-
Twin	1 to 8	C	1⅜"	6 each	896
	9 to 12	D	2⅝"	4 each	448
	13	A	4¾"	14	112
	13	B	2⅛"	12	448
	1st Border	-	2"	9	-
	2nd Border	-	3"	9	-
	3rd Border	-	4½"	9	-
Double	1 to 8	C	1⅜"	7 each	1120
	9 to 12	D	2⅝"	5 each	560
	13	A	4¾"	18	140
	13	B	2⅛"	15	560
	1st Border	-	1½"	10	-
	2nd Border	-	3½"	10	-
	3rd Border	-	5½"	10	-
Queen	1 to 8	C	1⅜"	10 each	1536
	9 to 12	D	2⅝"	6 each	768
	13	A	4¾"	24	192
	13	B	2⅛"	21	768
	1st Border	-	2½"	11	-
	2nd Border	-	4½"	11	-
	3rd Border	-	6½"	11	-
King	1 to 8	C	1⅜"	12 each	1792
	9 to 12	D	2⅝"	7 each	896
	13	A	4¾"	28	224
	13	B	2⅛"	24	896
	1st Border	-	2½"	12	-
	2nd Border	-	6½"	12	-

Cutting the Pieces

Cut the strips indicated on the "Cutting the Strips" chart.

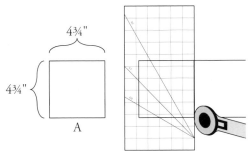

A Pieces. Divide the 4¾" strips of fabric #13 into squares.

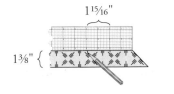

B Pieces. Divide the 2⅛" strips of fabric #13 into squares.

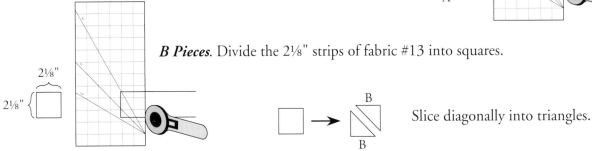

Slice diagonally into triangles.

C Pieces. Use the 1⅜" strips of fabrics #1 through #8. Take your ruler and lay the 45° line along the bottom edge of the strip as shown and cut the angle.

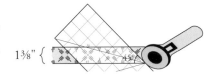

For this step you must use a ruler with ⅟₁₆" markings such as EZ's Draft 'n Cut Ruler. From edge, measure every 1¹⁵⁄₁₆" along the top of the strip and mark with a dot.

Lay the 45° angle on your ruler along the bottom edge of the strip with the cutting edge at the dot, and slice.

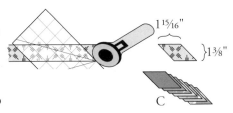

D Pieces. Divide the 2⅝" strips of fabrics #9 through #12 into squares.

Slice diagonally into triangles.

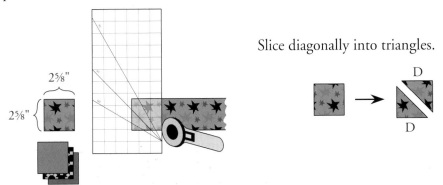

Assembling the Block

Sew sixteen **C/B/C** units, mixing fabrics. Add **D** pieces to **C/B/C** units.

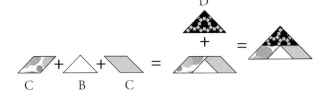

118

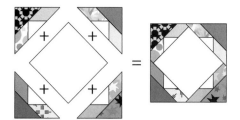

Sew completed **C/B/C/D** units on the sides of **A**.

Join squares as shown. Sew 2 halves together.

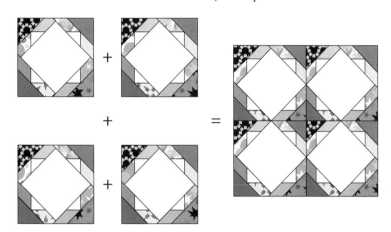

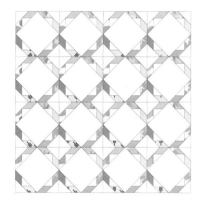

Follow the "Sewing the Quilt Top Together" section on pages 14-15 to complete your quilt top.

Variation: This quilt would also be very pretty if the background filled every area except the diamonds (piece **C**).

Fabric #1   Fabric #7

Fabric #2   Fabric #8

Fabric #3   Fabric #9

Fabric #4   Fabric #10

Fabric #5   Fabric #11

Fabric #6   Fabric #12

Fabric #13

Cross My Heart

This pattern makes an irresistible quilt or wallhanging with hearts coming out all over! We did the pattern with two different colored blocks alternating throughout the quilt – a rose combination and a red combination. Each block has two color variations within itself. See the blocks on page 125 for placement. You will need to pick out four different color combinations, two for each block.

You can use bold colors like we did (black, red and rose) or use soft pastels to create a whole different look. The darkest heart in each combination should be in the center, working out to light.

See photograph page 51.

Yardage Chart					
	Wall **3 x 3**	**Twin** **4 x 7**	**Double** **5 x 7**	**Queen** **6 x 8**	**King** **7 x 8**
Fabric #					
1	1/3	5/8	7/8	1	1 1/4
2	1/4	1/2	1/2	5/8	3/4
3	1/3	1/2	5/8	2/3	7/8
4	1/3	5/8	7/8	1	1 1/4
5	1/4	1/2	1/2	5/8	3/4
6	1/3	1/2	5/8	2/3	7/8
7	1/3	5/8	7/8	1	1 1/4
8	1/4	1/2	1/2	5/8	3/4
9	1/3	1/2	5/8	2/3	7/8
10	1/3	5/8	7/8	1	1 1/4
11	1/4	1/2	1/2	5/8	3/4
12	1/3	1/2	5/8	2/3	7/8
13	3/4	1 5/8	2	2 1/4	2 3/4
Borders (finished sizes given)					
1st Border (background)	1" – 1/3	1 1/2" – 1/2	1" – 1/2	2" – 7/8	2" – 7/8
2nd Border	2" – 1/2	2 1/2" – 3/4	3" – 1	4" – 1 1/2	6" – 2
3rd Border	4" – 1	4" – 1 1/8	5" – 1 5/8	6" – 2	-
Batting	3	6	6	6 1/4	9
Back	3	6	6 1/8	8	9
Binding	1	1	1	1	1 1/4
Finished Size	50" x 50"	64" x 100"	78" x 102"	84" x 108"	100" x 112"

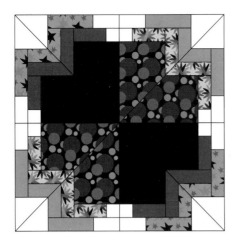

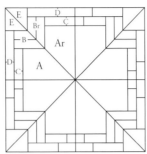

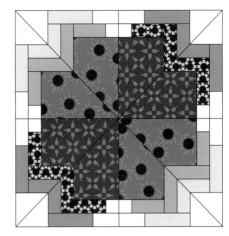

Cutting the Strips					
Quilt	Fabric #	Pattern Piece	Size of Strip	Number of Strips	Total Pieces Needed per Fabric
Wall	1, 4, 7, 10	A	3⅛"	2	20
	2, 5, 8, 11	Unit B	1¼"	2	20 units
	2, 5, 8, 11	Unit C	2⅜"	1	20 units
	3, 6, 9 ,12	Unit B	1¼"	2	20 units
	3, 6, 9 ,12	Unit D	3⅛"	1	20 units
	13	Unit C	1¼"	4	20 units
	13	Unit D	2"	4	20 units
	13	E	2¾"	3	80
	1st Border	-	1½"	6	-
	2nd Border	-	2½"	6	-
	3rd Border	-	4½"	6	-
Twin	1, 4, 7, 10	A	3⅛"	6	56
	2, 5, 8, 11	Unit B	1¼"	5	56 units
	2, 5, 8, 11	Unit C	2⅜"	2	56 units
	3, 6, 9 ,12	Unit B	1¼"	5	56 units
	3, 6, 9 ,12	Unit D	3⅛"	2	56 units
	13	Unit C	1¼"	8	56 units
	13	Unit D	2"	8	56 units
	13	E	2¾"	8	224
	1st Border	-	2"	9	-
	2nd Border	-	3"	9	-
	3rd Border	-	4½"	9	-

Cutting the Strips (continued)

Quilt	Fabric #	Pattern Piece	Size of Strip	Number of Strips	Total Pieces Needed per Fabric
Double	1, 4, 7, 10	A	3⅛"	8	72
	2, 5, 8, 11	Unit B	1¼"	6	72 units
	2, 5, 8, 11	Unit C	2⅜"	3	72 units
	3, 6, 9, 12	Unit B	1¼"	6	72 units
	3, 6, 9, 12	Unit D	3⅛"	3	72 units
	13	Unit C	1¼"	12	72 units
	13	Unit D	2"	12	72 units
	13	E	2¾"	10	280
	1st Border	-	1½"	10	-
	2nd Border	-	3½"	10	-
	3rd Border	-	5½"	10	-
Queen	1, 4, 7, 10	A	3⅛"	10	96
	2, 5, 8, 11	Unit B	1¼"	8	96 units
	2, 5, 8, 11	Unit C	2⅜"	3	96 units
	3, 6, 9, 12	Unit B	1¼"	8	96 units
	3, 6, 9, 12	Unit D	3⅛"	3	96 units
	13	Unit C	1¼"	12	96 units
	13	Unit D	2"	12	96 units
	13	E	2¾"	13	384
	1st Border	-	2½"	11	-
	2nd Border	-	4½"	11	-
	3rd Border	-	6½"	11	-
King	1, 4, 7, 10	A	3⅛"	12	112
	2, 5, 8, 11	Unit B	1¼"	10	112 units
	2, 5, 8, 11	Unit C	2⅜"	4	112 units
	3, 6, 9, 12	Unit B	1¼"	10	112 units
	3, 6, 9, 12	Unit D	3⅛"	4	112 units
	13	Unit C	1¼"	16	112 units
	13	Unit D	2"	16	112 units
	13	E	2¾"	15	448
	1st Border	-	2½"	12	-
	2nd Border	-	6½"	12	-

Cutting and Sewing the Pieces

Cut the strips indicated on the "Cutting the Strips" chart.

A Pieces. Note: To slice these pieces, open the strips and place two strips of the same fabric right sides together instead of folding the strips in half like you've been doing for most patterns. This exception is because of the fabric waste that occurs when strips are folded.

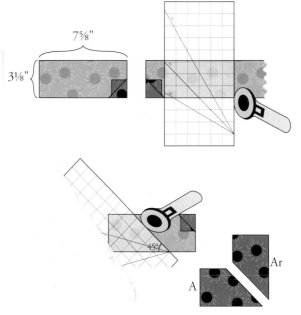

Divide the 3⅛" strips of fabrics #1, #4, #7 and into rectangles every 7⅝".

Keeping the rectangles in pairs, right sides together, measure along the rectangles and mark them at 5⅜" from the left edge. Lay the 45° line of your ruler on the bottom edge and slice. This will give you both **A** and **Ar** pieces.

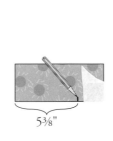

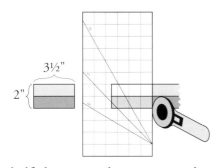

Unit B.

We call these units because the final piece contains two fabrics. You will use eight fabrics to make the following fabric combinations:

Fabrics #2 and #3   Fabrics #5 and #6   Fabrics #8 and #9   Fabrics #11 and #12

Lay the 1¼" strips of the above combinations right sides together and sew. Open and press seam to one side. Slice all units into rectangles every 3½".

With the darker strip on the bottom, lay the 45° line on your ruler at the bottom right edge and slice. Slice half the rectangles one way, then change the direction of the 45° ruler and slice the rest the opposite way to reverse the pieces.

Unit C.

The four fabric combinations for these units are:

Fabrics #2 and #13   Fabrics #5 and #13
Fabrics #8 and #13   Fabrics #11 and #13

You'll use the 2⅜" wide strips of fabrics #2, #5, #8 and #11 and the 1¼" wide strips of fabric #13.

Sew 2⅜" strips to 1¼" strips in pairs. Open and press seams toward the darker fabric. Slice every 1¼" to make rectangles.

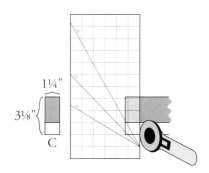

Unit D.

The four combinations for these units are:

Fabrics #3 and #13   Fabrics #6 and #13   Fabrics #9 and #13   Fabrics #12 and #13

You'll use the 3⅛" wide strips of fabrics # 3, #6, #9 and #12 and the 2" strips of fabric #13.

Sew 3⅛" strips to 2" strips in pairs. Open and press seams toward the darker fabric.

Slice these units every 1¼" to make rectangles.

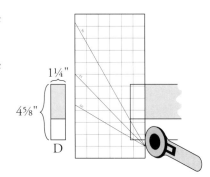

E Pieces. Divide the 2¾" strips of fabric #13 into squares.

Slice diagonally into triangles.

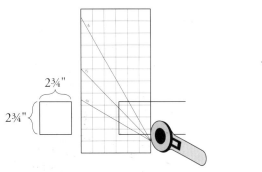

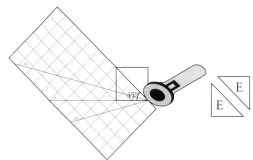

Assembling the Block

You will sew this block together in quarters. Follow the steps below to construct one-quarter of a block.

Sew unit **C** to piece A.   Sew unit **B** to that section.

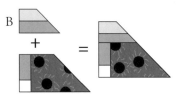

Add unit **D** next.   Piece **E** is joined to the top.

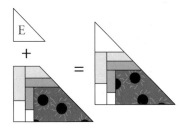

Repeat above steps for the other side using pieces **Ar** and Unit **Br**, and sew the two halves together.

Sew the quarters of the block together as shown.

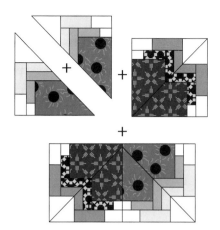

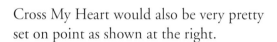

Follow the "Sewing the Quilt Top Together" section on pages 14-15 to complete your quilt top.

Cross My Heart would also be very pretty set on point as shown at the right.

"No Stress" Vest

See photograph page 63.

This vest not only looks great – it even uses up the 1" scraps of fabric you can't bear to throw away. Here is a great way to use all the little scraps generated from doing the quilt projects in this book!

Choose a simple vest pattern and we'll tell you the quick machine technique to make an absolutely wonderful vest in no time, with very little stress!

For this method you'll need:

- Fabric for vest and lining. Follow the requirements on your pattern for the vest and lining fabric. If your pattern does not show a lining, get enough fabric to line both front and back pieces.

- Sewing machine that goes forward and backward.

- 3 to 5 colors of thread to coordinate with scraps. Use some metallic thread if you like.

- Lots of scraps. Cut them into 1" to 2½" squares, rectangles, triangles, etc. For the back, armhole, and outside edging, you'll use all squares 1¾" to 2".

- Iron-on pellon (medium to light weight). Enough to cover vest fabric.

- Baste and Stick Glue. (The kind used on paper or fabric, not the hot glue.)

Practicing the Technique

To get comfortable with the crazy sewing technique, first let's make a sandwich out of scraps before you begin your vest.

To make the sandwich, cut two fabric squares about 5" x 5" and iron interfacing on one. Pin layers together. Take a few of your small scraps and arrange them so that they overlap on the front. Tack them down with a dab of glue from your glue stick.

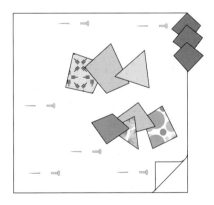

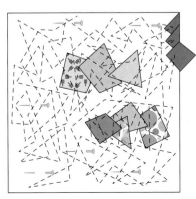

Thread your machine with one of the thread colors (your bobbin can be different). Place your needle in the middle of your piece and put the presser foot down. Begin with a backstitch and then sew forward a few inches. Now go backwards in another direction. Keep going forward and backwards, changing the angle each time. Practice guiding the fabric with your left hand and operating the reverse button with your right hand. You'll want to have stitching all over the square, changing thread colors often.

126

Hint: It takes longer to sew in reverse, so we usually do this so that most of the movement is forward: Sew backwards for a short time, then pivot and go forward again. After you feel comfortable practicing, you're ready to construct your vest.

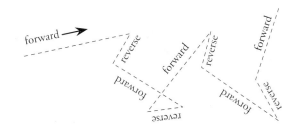

Cutting Out

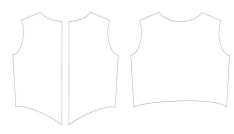

You will most likely have two front pieces and one back piece. Cut vest fabric, lining and iron-on interfacing from the same pattern pieces.

Iron the interfacing on to the wrong side of the vest pieces.

Layer the sections with the vest and lining pieces *wrong sides together*. Pin or hand baste layers together so they don't shift when you are machine sewing.

Constructing the Vest

Lay small fabric scraps on the right side of the background vest pieces and glue them in place. Sew patches on with the crazy sewing technique as explained above. Be sure and catch the edges and corners of the scraps in as many places as possible.

Change thread colors often, evenly distributing them over the vest.

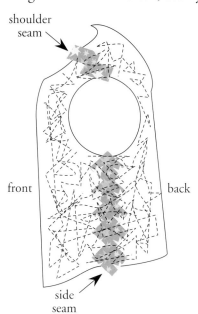

To finish shoulder and side seams, overlap them one at a time about ½" and pin. Sew scrap squares over the raw edges of all seams inside and outside of the vest using crazy sewing. Covering the inside seams will make your vest reversible. Sometimes it's nice to use all one color to do this or make it "scrappy" if you like.

Raw Edges. To finish the raw edges, overlap squares one at a time at an angle as you sew them on with crazy stitching. One half of the squares will be on the vest and the other half will hang over the edge. (We overlapped each square about ½".)

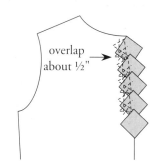

After sewing squares on all the edges, turn vest to the opposite side. Fold squares over the raw edge to the lining and sew again. For example, if you sewed squares on the outside of the vest first, then flip the second half of the squares to the lining side and sew again.

Wash and dry your vest to give it some character and it's ready to wear!